Praise for
THE REVOLUTION

"An indispensable guide to the thinking of an honorable American rebel who believes that those who preside over our fates on Capitol Hill have routinely betrayed the word and the spirit of the American Revolution."

—*New York Sun*

"One of those rare books that dares to tackle issues usually regarded as dauntingly complex (monetary policy in particular) and manages to render them in language both comprehensible and enjoyable to read . . . THE REVOLUTION is not a rant but an impassioned appeal. It is Dr. Paul at his principled, gentle-manly, scholarly best . . . A good manifesto needs to have a plan of action, not merely a statement of beliefs. And here Dr. Paul also delivers."

—*The New American*

"[Eight] concise and lucid chapters that never lose the thread of hope . . . he states his views strongly and then deals with the counterarguments his formulations invite . . . We should all take his manifesto seriously."

—*Washington Times*

THE
REVOLUTION
A Manifesto

Ron Paul

GRAND CENTRAL
PUBLISHING

NEW YORK   BOSTON

Grand Central Publishing
Hachette Book Group
237 Park Avenue
New York, NY 10017

Visit our website at www.HachetteBookGroup.com.

Printed in the United States of America

Originally published in hardcover by Grand Central Publishing.

First Trade Edition: September 2009
10   9   8   7   6   5   4   3   2   1

Grand Central Publishing is a division of Hachette Book Group, Inc.
The Grand Central Publishing name and logo is a trademark of
Hachette Book Group, Inc.

The Library of Congress cataloged the hardcover edition as follows:

Paul, Ron
  The revolution : a manifesto / Ron Paul.
    p.   cm.
  Summary: "Congressman Ron Paul (TX-R)—presidential candidate,
popular ideologue, debate favorite, and creator of one of the largest grassroots
campaigns in history—sets forth his revolutionary manifesto and challenges
America to make the tough changes needed to survive."—Provided by the
publisher.
    ISBN: 978-0-446-53751-3
    1. Paul, Ron, 1935–.   2. Presidential candidates—United States.
  3. United States—Politics and government—Philosophy.   4. United
  States—Politics and government—2001–.   5. Presidents—United States—
  Election—2008.   I. Title.
  E901.1.P38A3   2008
  973.931092—dc22
                                                          2008003293
  ISBN 978-0-446-53752-0 (pbk.)

To my supporters:
I have never been more humbled and honored than by
your selfless devotion to freedom and the Constitution.

The American Revolutionaries did the impossible.
So can we.

Contents

Preface

Every election cycle we are treated to candidates who promise us "change," and 2008 has been no different. But in the American political lexicon, "change" always means more of the same: more government, more looting of Americans, more inflation, more police-state measures, more unnecessary war, and more centralization of power.

Real change would mean something like the opposite of those things. It might even involve following our Constitution. And that's the one option Americans are never permitted to hear.

Today we are living in a fantasy world. Our entitlement programs are insolvent: in a couple of decades they will face a shortfall amounting to tens of trillions of dollars. Meanwhile, the housing bubble is bursting and our dollar is collapsing. We are borrowing billions from China every day in order to prop up a bloated overseas presence that weakens our national defense and stirs up hostility against us. And all our political class can come up with is more of the same.

One columnist puts it like this: we are borrowing from Europe in order to defend Europe, we are borrowing from Japan in order to keep cheap oil flowing to Japan, and we are borrowing from Arab regimes in order to install democracy in Iraq. Is it really "isolationism" to find something wrong with this picture?

With national bankruptcy looming, politicians from both parties continue to make multitrillion-dollar promises of "free" goods from the government, and hardly a soul wonders if we can still afford to have troops in—this is not a misprint—130 countries around the world. All of this is going to come to an end sooner or later, because financial reality is going to make itself felt in very uncomfortable ways. But instead of thinking about what this means for how we conduct our foreign and domestic affairs, our chattering classes seem incapable of speaking in anything but the emptiest platitudes, when they can be bothered to address serious issues at all. Fundamental questions like this, and countless others besides, are off the table in our mainstream media, which focuses our attention on trivialities and phony debates as we march toward oblivion.

This is the deadening consensus that crosses party lines, that dominates our major media, and that is strangling the liberty and prosperity that were once the birthright of Americans. Dissenters who tell their fellow citizens what is really going on are subject to smear campaigns that, like clockwork, are aimed at the political heretic. Truth is treason in the empire of lies.

There is an alternative to national bankruptcy, a bigger police state, trillion-dollar wars, and a government that draws ever more parasitically on the productive energies of the American people. It's called freedom. But as we've learned through hard experience, we are not going to hear a word in its favor if our political and media establishments have anything to say about it.

If we want to live in a free society, we need to break free from these artificial limitations on free debate and start asking serious questions once again. I am happy that my campaign for the presidency has finally raised some of them. But this is a long-term project that will persist far into the future. These ideas cannot be allowed to die, buried beneath the mind-numbing chorus of empty slogans and inanities that constitute official political discourse in America.

That is why I wrote this book.

THE
REVOLUTION

CHAPTER 1

The False Choices of
American Politics

Every election season America is presented with a series of false choices. Should we launch preemptive wars against this country or that one? Should every American neighborhood live under this social policy or that one? Should a third of our income be taken away by an income tax or a national sales tax? The shared assumptions behind these questions, on the other hand, are never cast in doubt, or even raised. And anyone who wants to ask different questions or who suggests that the questions as framed exclude attractive, humane alternatives, is ipso facto excluded from mainstream discussion.

And so every four years we are treated to the same tired, predictable routine: two candidates with few disagreements on fundamentals pretend that they represent dramatically different philosophies of government.

The supposedly conservative candidate tells us about "waste" in government, and ticks off $10 million in frivolous pork-barrel projects that outrage him—the inevitable bridge-to-nowhere project, or a study of the effects of celery consumption on arresting memory loss—in order to elicit laughter and applause from partisan audiences. All right, so that's 0.00045 percent of the federal budget dealt with; what does he propose to do with the other 99.99955 percent, in order to return our country to living within its means? Not a word. Those same three or four silly programs will be brought up all campaign long, and that's all we'll hear about where the candidate stands on spending. But conservatives are told that they must support these candidates, and so they do, hoping for the best. And nothing changes.

Even war doesn't really distinguish the two parties from each other. Hillary Clinton and John Kerry voted for the Iraq war. With the exceptions of Dennis Kucinich and Mike Gravel, even the Democrats who postured as antiwar candidates for the 2008 primary elections are not especially opposed to needless wars. They typically have a laundry list of other military interventions they would support, none of which make any sense, would make our country any safer, or would do a thing to return our country to fiscal sanity. But liberals are told that they must support these candidates, and so they do, hoping for the best. And nothing changes.

A substantial portion of the conservative movement has become a parody of its former self. Once home to distinguished intellectuals and men of letters, it now tolerates and even encourages anti-intellectualism and jingoism that would have embarrassed earlier generations of conservative thinkers. There are still some good and decent conservative leaders to be found, and a portion of the grass roots has remained uncorrupted by the transformation of conservatism into just another Big Government movement. But Big Government at home and abroad seems to suit many conservative spokesmen just fine. Once in a while they will latch on to phony but conservative-sounding causes like "tax reform"—almost always a shell game in which taxes are shuffled around rather than actually reduced overall—in order to pacify the conservative base, but that's about it.

When Republicans won a massive off-year election victory in 1994, neoconservative Bill Kristol immediately urged them not to do anything drastic but to wait until the Republicans took the White House in 1996. Well, the Republicans didn't take the White House in 1996, so nothing ever got done. Instead, the Republican leadership urged these freshman congressmen to focus on a toothless, soporific agenda called the Contract with America that was boldly touted as a major overhaul of the federal government. Nothing could have been further from the truth. The Contract with America was typical of what I have just described: no fundamental questions are ever raised, and even supposedly radical and revolutionary measures turn out to be modest and safe. In fact, the Brookings Institution in effect said that if *this* is what conservatives consider revolutionary, then they have basically conceded defeat.

Needless to say, I am also unimpressed by the liberal Left. Although they posture as critical thinkers, their confidence in government is inexcusably naive, based as it is on civics-textbook platitudes that bear absolutely zero resemblance to reality. Not even their position on unnecessary wars is consistent, as I noted above. Even Howard Dean was all in favor of Bill Clinton's intervention in Bosnia, going so far as to urge the president to take unilateral military action beyond the multilateral activity already taking place. Liberals at the grass roots, on the other hand, have been deeply alienated by the various betrayals by which a movement they once supported has made its peace with the establishment.

No wonder frustrated Americans have begun referring to our two parties as the Republicrats. And no wonder the news networks would rather focus on $400 haircuts than matters of substance. There *are* no matters of substance.

In late 2006, a number of friends and colleagues urged me to consider running for president. I was a reluctant candidate, not at all convinced that a sizable enough national constituency existed for a campaign based on liberty and the Constitution rather than on special-interest pandering and the distribution of loot.

Was I ever wrong.

On November 5, 2007, we set a record when we raised over $4 million online in a single day. That December 16, on the anniversary of the Boston Tea Party, we broke that record by raising over $6 million. In the fourth quarter of 2007, we raised more than twice as much money as any other Republican candidate. Not only is the freedom message popular, but if fundraising ability is any indication, it is more intensely popular than any other political message.

By the end of 2007, more than twice as many Meetup groups had been formed in support of our campaign than for all the rest of the candidates in both major parties combined. I have never seen such a diverse coalition rallying to a single banner. Republicans, Democrats, Independents, Greens, constitutionalists, whites, blacks, Hispanics, Asian-Americans, antiwar activists, homeschoolers, religious conservatives, freethinkers—all were not only involved, but enthusiastically so. And despite their philosophical differences in some areas, these folks typically found, to their surprise, that they rather liked each other.

The mainstream media had no idea what to make of it, since we were breaking all the rules and yet still attracting such a varied and passionate following. I began making this a central point of my public speeches: the reason all these different groups are rallying to the same banner, I said, is that freedom has a unique power to unite us.

In case that sounds like a cliché, it isn't. It's common sense. When we agree not to treat each other merely as means to our own selfish ends, but to respect one another as individuals with rights and goals of our own, cooperation and goodwill suddenly become possible for the first time.

My message is one of freedom and individual rights. I believe individuals have a right to life and liberty and that physical aggression should be used only defensively. We should respect each other as rational beings by trying to achieve our goals through reason and persuasion rather than threats and coercion. That, and not a desire for "economic efficiency," is the primary moral reason for opposing government intrusions into our lives: government is force, not reason.

People seem to think I am speaking of principles foreign to the Republican tradition. But listen to the words of Robert A. Taft, who in the old days of the Republican Party was once its standard-bearer:

When I say liberty I do not simply mean what is referred to as "free enterprise." I mean liberty of the individual to think his own thoughts and live his own life as he desires to think and to live; the liberty of the family to decide how they wish to live, what they want to eat for breakfast and for dinner, and how they wish to spend their time; liberty of a man to develop his ideas and get other people to teach those ideas, if he can convince them that they have some value to the

5

world; liberty of every local community to decide how its children shall be educated, how its local services shall be run, and who its local leaders shall be; liberty of a man to choose his own occupation; and liberty of a man to run his own business as he thinks it ought to be run, as long as he does not interfere with the right of other people to do the same thing.

As we'll see in a later chapter, Taft was also an opponent of needless wars and of unconstitutional presidential war-making.

This is the Republican tradition to which I belong.

Early on in my presidential campaign, people began describing my message and agenda as a "revolution." In a way, it is, albeit a peaceful one. In a country with a political debate as restricted as ours, it is revolutionary to ask whether we need troops in 130 countries and whether the noninterventionist foreign policy recommended by our Founding Fathers might not be better. It is revolutionary to ask whether the accumulation of more and more power in Washington has been good for us. It is revolutionary to ask fundamental questions about privacy, police-state measures, taxation, social policy, and countless other matters.

This revolution, though, is not altogether new. It is a peaceful continuation of the American Revolution and the principles of our Founding Fathers: liberty, self-government, the Constitution, and a noninterventionist foreign policy. That is what they taught us, and that is what we now defend.

I was never interested in writing a campaign book, as they tend to have (deservedly) short shelf lives. But the ideas I have been promoting, and which have struck such a powerful chord with so many Americans, are ideas that are overlooked and neglected because they do not fit into the template of trivial questions with which I opened this chapter. This book is an opportunity to highlight and explain them in the kind of systematic fashion that campaign speeches and presidential debates simply do not allow.

The revolution my supporters refer to will persist long after my retirement from politics. Here is my effort to give them a long-term manifesto based on ideas, and perhaps some short-term marching orders.

At the same time, I am also describing what the agenda of George W. Bush's successor should be if we want to move toward a free society once again. Our country is facing an unprecedented financial crisis precisely because the questions our political and media establishments allow us to ask are so narrow. Whether or not politicians actually want to hear them, it has never been more important for us to begin posing significant and fundamental questions. "In all affairs," Bertrand Russell once said, "it's a healthy thing now and then to hang a question mark on the things you have long taken for granted." I'm not in the habit of quoting Russell, but when in American history has his sentiment been more true?

CHAPTER 2

The Foreign Policy of the Founding Fathers

Our Founding Fathers gave us excellent advice on foreign policy. Thomas Jefferson, in his first inaugural address, called for "peace, commerce, and honest friendship with all nations, entangling alliances with none." George Washington, several years earlier, took up this theme in his Farewell Address. "Harmony, liberal intercourse with all nations, are recommended by policy, humanity, and interest," he maintained. "But even our commercial policy should hold an equal and impartial hand; neither seeking nor granting exclusive favors or preferences." Washington added:

> The great rule of conduct for us in regard to foreign nations is in extending our commercial relations, to have with them as little political connection as possible. . . . Why quit our own to stand upon foreign ground? Why, by interweaving our destiny with that of any part of Europe, entangle our peace and prosperity in the toils of European ambition, rivalship, interest, humor or caprice?

Unfortunately, we have spent the past century spurning this sensible advice. If the Founders' advice is acknowledged at all, it is dismissed on the grounds that we no longer live in their times. The same hackneyed argument could be used against any of the other principles the Founders gave us. Should we give up the First Amendment because times have changed? How about the rest of the Bill of Rights? It's hypocritical and childish to dismiss certain founding principles simply because a convenient rationale is needed to justify foolish policies today. The principles enshrined in the Constitution do not change. If anything, today's more complex world cries out for the moral clarity of a noninterventionist foreign policy.

It is easy to dismiss the noninterventionist view as the quaint aspiration of men who lived in a less complicated world, but it's not so easy to demonstrate how our current policies serve any national interest at all. Perhaps an honest examination of the history of American interventionism in the twentieth century, from Korea to Vietnam to Kosovo to the Middle East, would reveal that the Founding Fathers foresaw more than we think.

Anyone who advocates the noninterventionist foreign policy of the Founding Fathers can expect to be derided as an isolationist. I myself have never been an isolationist. I favor the very opposite of isolation: diplomacy, free trade, and freedom of travel. The real isolationists are those who impose sanctions and embargoes on countries and peoples across the globe because they disagree with the internal and foreign policies of their leaders. The real isolationists are those who choose to use force overseas to promote democracy, rather than seeking change through diplomacy, engagement, and by setting a positive example. The real isolationists are those who isolate their country in the court of world opinion by pursuing needless belligerence and war that have nothing to do with legitimate national security concerns.

Interestingly enough, George W. Bush sounded some of these themes when he ran for president in the year 2000. By that time, many Republicans had grown weary of Bill Clinton's military interventions and forays into nation building and wanted to put a stop to it. Sensibly enough, Bush spoke of a humble foreign policy, no nation building, and no policing the world. In 1999, then Governor Bush declared: "Let us have an American foreign policy that reflects American character. The modesty of true strength. The humility of real greatness."

In a debate with Vice President Al Gore the following year, Bush said: "I'm not so sure the role of the United States is to go around the world and say, 'This is the way it's got to be.' . . . I think one way for us to end up being viewed as 'the ugly American' is for us to go around the world saying, 'We do it this way; so should you.'"

Bush also rejected nation building. "Somalia started off as a humanitarian mission and changed into a nation-building mission," he said. "And that's where the mission went wrong. The mission was changed. And as a result, our nation paid a price. And so I don't think our troops ought to be used for what's called 'nation building.'" He added, "I think what we need to do is to convince the people who live in the lands [themselves] to build the nations. Maybe I'm missing something here—we're going to have kind of a 'nation-building corps' from America?"

Finally, when discussing other countries' perception of the United States, Bush said: "If we're an arrogant nation, they'll resent us. If we're a humble nation, but strong, they'll welcome us. Our nation stands alone right now in the world in terms of power, and that's why we've got to be humble." We should be "proud and confident [in] our values, but humble in how we treat nations that are figuring out how to chart their own course."

In other words, President Bush ran and won on a very different foreign policy from the one we are told all Republicans must support. We know what came later, of course. And by the 2008 Republican primaries, one of the front-runners had strayed so far from President Bush's original platform that he was even saying that in the future, nation building should become one of the standard functions of the American military.

Some Americans may be familiar with the admonition of John Quincy Adams that America does not go abroad in search of monsters to destroy. But his sentiments extended well beyond this oft-cited maxim. First, Adams considered what could be said in America's defense if anyone were ever to wonder what she had done for the world:

> [I]f the wise and learned philosophers of the elder world . . . should find their hearts disposed to enquire what has America done for the benefit of mankind? Let our answer be this: America, with the same voice which spoke herself into existence as a nation, proclaimed to mankind the inextinguishable rights of human nature, and the only lawful foundations of government. America, in the assembly of nations, since her admission among them, has invariably, though often fruitlessly, held forth to them the hand of honest friendship, of equal freedom, of generous reciprocity. She has uniformly spoken among them, though often to heedless, and often to disdainful ears, the language of equal liberty, of equal justice, and of equal rights; she has,

in the lapse of nearly half a century, without a single exception, respected the independence of other nations while asserting and maintaining her own; she has abstained from interference in the concerns of others, even when the conflict has been for principles to which she clings as to the last vital drop that visits the heart.

Adams then described the foreign policy of the American republic:

Wherever the standard of freedom and Independence has been or shall be unfurled, there will her heart, her benedictions and her prayers be. But she goes not abroad in search of monsters to destroy. She is the well-wisher to the freedom and independence of all. She is the champion and vindicator only of her own. She will commend the general cause by the countenance of her voice, and the benignant sympathy of her example. She well knows that by once enlisting under other banners than her own, were they even the banners of foreign independence, she would involve herself beyond the power of extrication, in all the wars of interest and intrigue, of individual avarice, envy, and ambition, which assume the colors and usurp the standard of freedom. The fundamental maxims of her policy would insensibly change from liberty to force. . . . She might become the dictatress of the world. She would be no longer the ruler of her own spirit. . . .

This wasn't "isolationism." It was a beautiful and elegant statement of common sense, and of principles that at one time were taken for granted by nearly everyone.

In the same way, Henry Clay was merely repeating George Washington's wise sentiments, rather than giving voice to isolationism, when he urged this piece of advice upon his countrymen: "By the policy to which we have adhered since the days of Washington . . . we have done more for the cause of liberty than arms could effect; we have shown to other nations the way to greatness and happiness. . . . Far better is it for ourselves . . . and the cause of liberty, that, adhering to our pacific system and avoiding the distant wars of Europe, we should keep our lamp burning brightly on this western shore, as a light to all nations, than to hazard its utter extinction amid the ruins of fallen and falling republics in Europe." Thus we should strive to lead by example rather than force, and provide a model for the world that other peoples will wish to follow. We do no one any good by bankrupting ourselves.

Richard Cobden was a nineteenth-century British statesman who opposed all of his government's foreign interventions. In those days, though, people understood the philosophy of nonintervention much better than they do today, and no one was silly enough to brand Cobden an isolationist. He was known instead, appropriately enough, as the International Man.

There are those who condemn noninterventionists for being insufficiently ambitious, for their unwillingness to embrace "national greatness"—as if a nation's greatness could be measured according to any calculus other than the virtues of its people and the excellence of its institutions. These critics should have the honesty to condemn the Founding Fathers for the same defect. They wouldn't dare. But it would be refreshing to hear it stated in so many words: our current political class is blessed with historic genius, and Jefferson, Washington, and Madison were contemptible fools.

What the Founding Fathers have to teach us about foreign policy became all the more important, and yet all the more ignored, in the wake of the horrific attacks of September 11, 2001.

In the weeks that followed that fateful day, most Americans' focus was on identifying the sponsors of the attacks and punishing them. That was sensible enough. I myself voted to track down al Qaeda in Afghanistan. But people were bound to start wondering, eventually, why we were attacked—not because they sought to excuse the attackers, of course, but out of a natural curiosity regarding what made these men tick. Looking for motive is not the same thing as making excuses; detectives always look for the motive behind crime, but no one thinks they are looking to excuse murder.

Seven years later, though, our political class still refuses to deal with the issue in anything but sound bites and propaganda. The rest of the world is astonished at this refusal to speak frankly about the reality of our situation. And yet our safety and security may depend on it.

One person to consult if we want to understand those who wish us harm is Michael Scheuer, who was chief of the CIA's Osama bin Laden Unit at the Counterterrorist Center in the late 1990s. Scheuer is a conservative and a pro-life voter who has never voted for a Democrat. And he refuses to buy the usual line that the attacks on America have nothing to do with what our government does in the Islamic world. "In fact," he says, those attacks have "everything to do with what we do."

Some people simply will not listen to this kind of argument, or will pretend to misunderstand it, trivializing this profoundly significant issue by alleging that Scheuer is "blaming America" for the attacks. To the contrary, Scheuer could not be any clearer in his writing that the perpetrators of terrorist attacks on Americans should be pursued mercilessly for their acts of barbarism. His point is very simple: it is unreasonable, even utopian, not to expect people to grow resentful, and desirous of revenge, when your government bombs them, supports police states in their countries, and imposes murderous sanctions on them. That revenge, in its various forms, is what our CIA calls blowback—the unintended consequences of military intervention.

Obviously the onus of blame rests with those who perpetrate acts of terror, regardless of their motivation. The question Scheuer and I are asking is not who is morally responsible for terrorism—only a fool would place the moral responsibility for terrorism on anyone other than the terrorists themselves. The question we are asking is less doltish and more serious: given that a hyper-interventionist foreign policy is very likely to lead to this kind of blowback, are we still sure we want such a foreign policy? Is it really worth it to us? The main focus of our criticism, in other words, is that our government's foreign policy has put the American people in greater danger and made us more vulnerable to attack than we would otherwise have been. *This* is the issue that we and others want to raise before the American people.

The interventionist policies that have given rise to blowback have been bipartisan in their implementation. For instance, it was Bill Clinton's secretary of state, Madeleine Albright, who said on *60 Minutes* that half a million dead Iraqi children as a result of the sanctions on that country during the 1990s were "worth it." Who could be so utopian, so detached from reality, as to think a remark like that—which was broadcast all over the Arab world, you can be sure—and policies like these would not provoke a response? If *Americans* lost that many of their family members, friends, and fellow citizens, would they not seek to hunt down the perpetrators and be unsatisfied until they were apprehended? The question answers itself. So why *wouldn't* we expect people to try to take revenge for these policies? I have never received an answer to this simple and obvious question.

This does not mean Americans are bad people, or that they are to blame for terrorism—straw-man arguments that supporters of intervention raise in order to cloud the issue and demonize their opponents. It means only that actions cause reactions, and that Americans will need to prepare themselves for these reactions if their government is going to continue to intervene around the world. In the year 2000, I wrote: "The cost in terms of liberties lost and the unnecessary exposure to terrorism are difficult to determine, but in time it will become apparent to all of us that foreign interventionism is of no benefit to American citizens, but instead is a threat to our liberties." I stand by every word of that.

To those who say that the attackers are motivated by a hatred of Western liberalism or the moral degeneracy of American culture, Scheuer points out that Iran's Ayatollah Khomeini tried in vain for a decade to instigate an anti-Western jihad on exactly that basis. It went nowhere. Bin Laden's message, on the other hand, has been so attractive to so many people because it is fundamentally defensive. Bin Laden, says Scheuer, has "spurned the Ayatollah's wholesale condemnation of Western society," focusing instead on "specific, bread-and-butter issues on which there is widespread agreement among Muslims."

What bin Laden's sympathizers object to, as they have said again and again, is our government's propping up of unpopular regimes in the Middle East, the presence of American troops on the Arabian Peninsula, the American government's support for the activities of governments (like Russia) that are hostile to their Muslim populations, and what they believe to be an American bias toward Israel. The point is not that we need to agree with these arguments, but that we need to be aware of them if we want to understand what is motivating so many people to rally to bin Laden's banner. Few people are moved to leave behind their worldly possessions and their families to carry out violence on behalf of a disembodied ideology; it is practical grievances, perhaps combined with an underlying ideology, that motivate large numbers to action.

At a press conference I held at the National Press Club in May 2007, Scheuer told reporters: "About the only thing that can hold together the very loose coalition that Osama bin Laden has assembled is a common Muslim hatred for the impact of U.S. foreign policy. . . . They all agree they hate U.S. foreign policy. To the degree we change that policy in the interests of the United States, they become more and more focused on their local problems." That's not what a lot of our talking heads tell us on television every day, but few people are in a better position to understand bin Laden's message than Scheuer, one of our country's foremost experts on the man.

Philip Giraldi, another conservative and former counterterrorism expert with the CIA, adds that "anybody who knows anything about what's been going on for the last ten years would realize that cause and effect are operating here—that, essentially, al Qaeda has an agenda which very specifically says what its grievances are. And its grievances are basically that 'we're over there.'" The simple fact is that "there [are] consequences for our presence in the Middle East, and if we seriously want to address the terrorism problem we have to be serious about that issue."

Even Deputy Secretary of Defense Paul Wolfowitz recognized that foreign intervention could have unintended consequences and that the American presence in the Middle East had bred hostility against our country. On May 29, 2003, Reuters reported: "Wolfowitz said another reason for the invasion [of Iraq] had been 'almost unnoticed but huge'—namely that the ousting of Saddam would allow the United States to remove its troops from Saudi Arabia, where their presence had long been a major al-Qaeda grievance." In short, according to Wolfowitz one of the motivations of the 9/11 attackers was resentment over the presence of American troops on the Arabian Peninsula. Again, neither Wolfowitz nor I have ever said or believed that Americans had it coming on 9/11, or that the attacks were justified, or any of this other nonsense. The point is a simple one: when our government meddles around the world, it can stir up hornet's nests and thereby jeopardize the safety of the American people. That's just common sense. But hardly anyone in our government dares to level with the American people about our fiasco of a foreign policy.

Blowback should not be a difficult or surprising concept for conservatives and libertarians, since they often emphasize the unintended consequences that even the most well-intentioned *domestic* program can have. We can only imagine how much greater and unpredictable the consequences of intervention abroad might be.

A classic example of blowback involves the overthrow of Prime Minister Muhammad Mossadegh in Iran in 1953. American and British intelligence collaborated on the overthrow of Mossadegh's popularly elected government, replacing him with the politically reliable but repressive shah. Years later, a revolutionary Iranian government took American citizens hostage for 444 days. There is a connection here—not because supporters of radical Islam would have had much use for the secular Mossadegh, but because on a human level people resent that kind of interference in their affairs.

When it comes to suicide bombing, I, like many others, always assumed that the driving force behind the practice was Islamic fundamentalism. Promise of instant entry into paradise as a reward for killing infidels was said to explain the suicides. The world's expert on suicide terrorism convinced me to rethink this apparently plausible answer. The University of Chicago's Robert Pape, for his book *Dying to Win: The Strategic Logic of Suicide Terrorism*, collected a database of all 462 suicide terrorist attacks between 1980 and 2004. One thing he found was that religious beliefs were less important as motivating factors than we have believed. The world's leaders in suicide terrorism are actually the Tamil Tigers in Sri Lanka, a Marxist secular group. The largest Islamic fundamentalist countries have not been responsible for any suicide terrorist attacks. Not one has come from Iran or the Sudan.

The clincher is this: the strongest motivation, according to Pape, is not religion but rather a desire "to compel modern democracies to withdraw military forces from the territory the terrorists view as their homeland." Between 1995 and 2004, the al Qaeda years, two-thirds of all attacks came from countries where the United States had troops stationed. While al Qaeda terrorists are twice as likely to hail from a country with a strong Wahhabist (radical Islamic) presence, they are ten times as likely to come from a country in which U.S. troops are stationed. Until the U.S. invasion in 2003, Iraq had never had a suicide terrorist attack in its entire history. Between 1982 and 1986, there were 41 suicide terrorist attacks in Lebanon. Once the U.S., France, and Israel withdrew their forces from Lebanon, there were no more attacks. The reason the attacks stop, according to Pape, is that the Osama bin Ladens of the world can no longer inspire potential suicide terrorists, regardless of their religious beliefs.

Pape is convinced after his extensive research that the longer and more extensive the occupation of Muslim territories, the greater the chance of more 9/11-type attacks on the United States.

Although most Americans don't know it, for much of the early twentieth century our country had an excellent reputation in the Middle East, the part of the world we are now told will hate us no matter what we do. Right now, after decades of meddling, our government is hated in the Middle East and around the world to a degree I have never before seen in my lifetime. That does not make us safer.

To be sure, there will always be those who wish us ill regardless of the foreign policy we adopt. But those who would recruit large numbers of their coreligionists to carry out violence against Americans find their task very difficult when they cannot point to some tangible issue that will motivate people to do so. It is bin Laden's specific list of grievances that has rallied so many to his cause. Predictably enough, al Qaeda recruitment has exploded since the invasion of Iraq.

The war in Iraq was one of the most ill-considered, poorly planned, and just plain unnecessary military conflicts in American history, and I opposed it from the beginning. But the beginning I am speaking of was not 2002 or 2003. As early as 1997 and 1998, shortly after my return to Congress after a dozen years back in my medical practice, I spoke out against the actions of the Clinton administration, which I believed was moving us once again toward war with Iraq. I believe the genesis of our later policy was being set at that time. Many of the same voices who then demanded that the Clinton administration attack Iraq later demanded that the Bush administration attack Iraq, exploiting the tragedy of September 11 to bring about their long-standing desire to see an American invasion of that country. Any rationale would do: "weapons of mass destruction," the wickedness of Saddam (an issue that did not seem to keep many of these policymakers up at night in the 1980s, when they were supporting him), a Saddam–al Qaeda link, whatever. As long as their Middle Eastern ambitions could be satisfied, it did not matter how the people were brought along.

By any standard—constitutional, financial, national defense—I could not see the merits of the proposed invasion of Iraq. Any serious Middle East observer could have told us, if we were listening, that Iraq had essentially no connection to terrorism. (At the time of the Persian Gulf War of 1991, Osama bin Laden actually offered to lead an army to defend Saudi Arabia against Saddam if necessary.) Iraq had not attacked us, and figures in our own government, including Condoleezza Rice and Colin Powell, had said that Saddam was effectively contained and no threat to anyone. Saddam's was not even an Islamic regime; it was a secular one—although, thanks to the war, that is now changing.

Some war apologists to this day still try to argue that the weapons were really there or that Saddam really was linked to al Qaeda, but I'm not sure why they bother. The administration long ago gave up on these claims.

In the midst of all this, it is essential not to lose sight of the moral dimension of war, and the lengths to which Christian and later secular thinkers have gone over the centuries to limit and restrict the waging of war. For well over a thousand years there has been a doctrine and Christian definition of what constitutes a just war. This just-war tradition developed in the fourth century with Ambrose and Augustine but grew to maturity with Thomas Aquinas and such Late Scholastics as Francisco de Vitoria and Francisco Suarez. The requirements for a just war varied to some extent from commentator to commentator, but those who wrote on the subject shared some basic principles. The war in Iraq did not even come close to satisfying them.

First, there has to be an initial act of aggression, in response to which a just war may be waged. But there was no act of aggression against the United States. We are 6,000 miles from Iraq. The phony stories we were told about unmanned drones coming to get us were, to say the least, not especially plausible.

Second, diplomatic solutions had not been exhausted. They had hardly been tried.

Traditional just-war criteria also demand that the initiation of war be undertaken by the proper authority. Under the U.S. Constitution, the proper authority is neither the president nor the United Nations. It is Congress—but Congress unconstitutionally delegated its decision-making power over war to the president.

I heard it argued that Saddam had indeed committed an act of aggression against the United States: he had shot at our airplanes. Those American planes were monitoring the "no-fly zones" over Iraq. Authority for such zones was said to come from U.N. Resolution 688, which instructs nations to contribute to humanitarian relief in the Kurdish and Shiite areas. The resolution actually says nothing about no-fly zones, and nothing about bombing missions over Iraq.

That Saddam Hussein missed every single airplane for 12 years as tens of thousands of sorties were being flown indicates the utter weakness of our enemy: an impoverished Third World nation that lacked an air force, antiaircraft weapons, and a navy. This was supposed to be the great threat, requiring urgent action. Such nonsense insults the intelligence of the American people and makes the rest of the world wonder about our sanity.

And yet the propaganda continues even today. In one of the Republican presidential debates, after being called an isolation-ist—honestly, is the distinction between isolationism and nonin-terventionism really so difficult to grasp?—I was solemnly informed that the course I recommended in Iraq amounted to the same kind of thinking that had led to Hitler! Now, all of us are used to hearing political propaganda, especially in presidential debates, but this really took the cake: were the American people expected to believe that unless they supported the invasion and occupation of a completely paralyzed Third World country, they were the sort of people who would have given aid and comfort to Hitler? Did this candidate really have such a low estimate of the intelligence of the American people?

How, after all, had Hitler been able to rise to power in the first place? Hitler made a name for himself by denouncing the Treaty of Versailles, which established the peace terms with Germany at the end of World War I. Many observers at the time and since have described the treaty as severe and one-sided. (And no, that is not how all postwar treaties are: after the Napoleonic Wars, the last continent-wide conflict until World War I, the Congress of Vienna imposed reasonable terms on defeated France and fully welcomed her back into the community of nations within only a few years.) Hitler appealed directly to this sense of grievance on the part of the German people: how long, he asked, are we going to allow ourselves to be treated like a third-class nation?

Now let us recall President Woodrow Wilson's decision to involve the United States in World War I. (The level of popular support for Wilson's decision may perhaps be gauged by the massive propaganda campaign, without precedent in American history, that the government undertook to win over public opinion.) The war in Europe had been a stalemate prior to Wilson's intervention. Thanks to that intervention, not only did the Allies win, but they were also now in a position to impose the punitive Versailles Treaty on a defeated Germany. It is not at all a stretch to say, as many historians have indeed said, that Wilson's decision to intervene gave inadvertent impetus to Hitler's politics of extreme nationalism, since the treaty it made possible helped catapult him into the limelight. Hitler might otherwise have remained a nobody. German president Paul von Hindenburg was said to have sized him up as potentially a good postmaster general.

Did Wilson *intend* this outcome? Did he intend to hand Hitler and his party a perfect strategy for their political advancement? Of course not. But here we are, faced once again with the unpredictability of foreign intervention, and the strong possibility that by removing a bad government we may wind up not with a better one, but a far worse one.

Ever since then, no libertarian or traditional conservative I am aware of has had anything but contempt for the utopian Wilson. The mainstream Left of his day was largely disillusioned by the outcome, having hoped for a more just peace, and genuine progressives like Robert La Follette, Randolph Bourne, and Jane

Addams had opposed the war from the beginning. That essentially leaves a smattering of neoconservatives today as Wilson's remaining defenders. But here was a historical lesson to learn if there ever was one.

The Iraq war is sometimes portrayed as a conservative/liberal issue. It isn't. Supporters of war and empire come from both political parties and can be found among both liberals and conservatives. The "liberal media" supported the Iraq war with enthusiasm, and in their eagerness to parrot the official line abandoned whatever critical faculties they possessed. The American media were so derelict in their duty during the Iraq war that one watchdog group actually offered a $1,000 reward for any reporter who would ask the administration a challenging question about prewar intelligence. Hillary Clinton was a strong supporter of the war. Following the off-year election in 2006, congressional Democrats, for the most part, revealed themselves once again to be a sorry excuse for an opposition party, continuing to fund the war and refusing to take any bold action.

———

For much of 2006 and 2007, it looked as if we were in for a repeat performance: propaganda and slogans, parroted by the media, threatened to take us to war yet again.

Then things changed. In December 2007, a National Intelligence Estimate compiled by sixteen agencies of the American intelligence apparatus concluded that Iran had discontinued its nuclear weapons program in 2003 and had not resumed it. Up until the very moment that report was issued, the so-called liberal media had been serving once again as uncritical mouthpieces of administration war propaganda, providing cover for yet another costly and avoidable conflict. This would never happen again, reporters and editorial writers assured us after the Iraq fiasco. Ten minutes later, they were back to their usual collusion with the political establishment.

I had said all along that Iran posed no imminent nuclear threat to us or to her neighbors, and now the intelligence community had confirmed that view—a view anyone who read newspapers outside the United States would have been informed enough to take for granted. The administration's rhetoric, on the other hand, gave the impression that nothing had changed. And from the administration's perspective nothing *had* changed, since it had apparently possessed this intelligence report for months, only making it known to the public in early December.

The administration's awkward efforts to cope with this new information tied it up in logical and rhetorical knots. First, administration officials tried to discredit the report, even though it was one of the most comprehensive intelligence reports on the subject, complete with over a thousand source notes. They then claimed that Iran's 2003 abandonment of its weapons program—a fact they drew from the supposedly faulty report—showed that American pressure must have worked, since Iran backed off from developing nuclear weapons just as the United States was invading Iraq. Our government must therefore keep up the pressure by means of yet another round of sanctions. Russia and China did not buy this analysis, and once again our isolationists in Washington placed America on a lonely and tenuous platform on the world stage.

As with Iraq, Iran has been asked to perform the logically impossible feat of proving a negative. Iran is presumed guilty until proven innocent because there is no evidence with which to indict. There is still no evidence that Iran, a signatory of the Nuclear Non-Proliferation Treaty, has ever violated the treaty's terms— terms which state that Iran is allowed to pursue nuclear energy for peaceful, civilian energy needs. The United States cannot unilaterally change the terms of that treaty, and it is unfair and unwise diplomatically to impose sanctions for no legitimate reason.

Iran, incidentally, may have noticed a pattern: if countries do have a nuclear weapon, they tend to be left alone, or possibly even given a subsidy. If they do not gain such a weapon they find themselves threatened with war. With that kind of foreign policy, what country wouldn't want to pursue a nuclear weapon? But in fact there is no evidence Iran actually has one, or could have one anytime soon, even if it immediately resumed a weapons program.

Still, when individuals want a war, any pretext will do, so the NIE report does not guarantee that our government will keep its hands off Iran. In the late summer of 2007, with the administration aware that the evidence for an Iranian nuclear weapons program was on the verge of collapse, President Bush signed an executive order designating Iran's elite 125,000-strong Revolutionary Guard Corps as a "terrorist" group, thereby establishing a new pretext for an attack on Iran. Fewer Americans are likely to accept that as a rationale for war than an Iranian nuclear weapon. The National Intelligence Estimate, if not ruling out the possibility of war, will at least make it more difficult to sell.

———

Neoconservatives, the false conservatives who got us into the Iraq mess and pushed hard for war with Iran, continue to hold their positions of prominence. Why that is so is quite beyond me. Every last prediction they made about the Iraq debacle—e.g., it would be a cakewalk, the cost would be paid by oil revenues, the prospect of sectarian fighting was slim—has been resolutely falsified by events, and yet they continue to grace the pages of major American newspapers and appear regularly on cable television talk shows. Instead of being disgraced, as common sense might lead us to expect, they continue to be exalted for a wisdom they obviously do not possess. I am reminded of George Orwell's reference to "the streamlined men who think in slogans and talk in bullets."

Meanwhile, where is the exposure for those who favor a non-interventionist foreign policy? These individuals would have avoided the Iraq fiasco altogether. America would be trillions richer over the long term, Iraqi society would not be in shambles, and countless Americans and Iraqis alike would still be alive. Noninterventionists have been entirely vindicated. And yet they do not enjoy the places of prominence that the establishment has bestowed on those who have been consistently wrong, and responsible for carnage and destruction that have destroyed our good name around the world and isolated us more than ever in our history. In fact, they are scarcely to be found at all.

Although you'd never know it by reading the print media or watching television talk shows, we who support the foreign policy of the Founding Fathers hold an honored place in the history of the Republican Party and of the conservative and libertarian movements. The so-called old Right, or original Right, opposed Big Government at home and abroad and considered foreign interventionism to be the other side of the same statist coin as interventionism at home. They recognized that Big Government was no more honest or competent in foreign policy than it was in domestic policy. In both cases it was the same institution, with the same people, operating under the same incentives.

A recent article in *Modern Age*, the conservative journal founded by Russell Kirk, illustrated this point. Felix Morley, for example, was one of the founders of *Human Events*, the oldest conservative weekly in America. In 1957 he wrote an essay called "American Republic or American Empire." There Morley warned, "We are trying to make a federal republic do an imperial job, without honestly confronting the fact that our traditional institutions are specifically designed to prevent centralization of power. . . . At some time and at some point, however, this fundamental conflict between our institutions and our policies will have to be resolved."

In *Freedom and Federalism*, Morley quoted Adolf Hitler as saying that "a powerful national government may encroach considerably upon the liberty of individuals as well as of the different States, and assume the responsibility for it, without weakening the Empire Idea, if only every citizen recognizes such measures as means for making his nation greater." Morley then elaborated on what Hitler meant:

> In other words, the problem of empire-building is essentially mystical. It must somehow foster the impression that a man is great in the degree that his nation is great; that a German as such is superior to a Belgian as such; an Englishman, to an Irishman; an American, to a Mexican: merely because the first-named countries are in each case more powerful than their comparatives. And people who have no individual stature whatsoever are willing to accept this poi-

sonous nonsense because it gives them a sense of importance without the trouble of any personal effort.

The phenomenon Morley describes could not be further removed from the ideas of republican government, which have grown foreign to us after decades of military overstretch.

Russell Kirk was one of the chief founders of American conservatism, and his book *The Conservative Mind* has been one of its most influential texts. And he, too, was suspicious of militarism: he was a critic of high military spending and opposed the Vietnam War, albeit privately. By the 1990s he was an outspoken opponent of his government's military interventions and was concerned that they were making his country unnecessary enemies. "Presidents Woodrow Wilson, Franklin Roosevelt, and Lyndon Johnson were enthusiasts for American domination of the world," Kirk said in 1991 at the Heritage Foundation. "Now George [H. W.] Bush appears to be emulating those eminent Democrats. . . . In general, Republicans throughout the twentieth century have been advocates of prudence and restraint in the conduct of foreign affairs."

As for wars for "democracy," Kirk—being the traditional conservative he was—could hardly take the idea seriously. "Are we to saturation-bomb most of Africa and Asia into righteousness, freedom, and democracy?" Kirk wondered. "And, having accomplished that, however would we ensure persons yet more unrighteous might not rise up instead of the ogres we had swept away? Just that is what happened in the Congo, remember, three decades ago; and nowadays in Zaire, once called the Belgian Congo, we zealously uphold with American funds the dictator Mobutu, more blood-stained than Saddam. And have we forgotten Castro in Cuba?"

In his book *The Political Principles of Robert A. Taft*, which he wrote with James McClellan, Kirk noted his subject's aversion to war. (Taft was the great exemplar of the old Right in the Senate in the 1940s and 1950s.) "War, Taft perceived, was the enemy of constitution, liberty, economic security, and the cake of custom. . . . Though he was no theoretical pacifist, he insisted that every other possibility must be exhausted before resort to military action. War would make the American President a virtual dictator, diminish the constitutional powers of Congress, contract civil liberties, injure the habitual self-reliance and self-government of the American people, distort the economy, sink the federal govenrment in debt, break in upon private and public morality." He went on:

> Taft's prejudice in favor of peace was equaled in strength by his prejudice against empire. Quite as the Romans had acquired an empire in a fit of absence of mind, he feared that America might make herself an imperial power with the best of intentions—and the worst of results. He foresaw the grim possibility of American garrisons in distant corners of the world, a vast permanent military establishment, an intolerant "democratism" imposed in the name of the American way of life, neglect of America's domestic concerns in the pursuit of transoceanic power, squandering of American resources upon amorphous international designs, the decay of liberty at home in proportion as America presumed to govern the world: that is, the "garrison state," a term he employed more than once. The record of the United States

as administrator of territories overseas had not been heartening, and the American constitution made no provision for a widespread and enduring imperial government. Aspiring to redeem the world from all the ills to which flesh is heir, Americans might descend, instead, into a leaden imperial domination and corruption.

Richard Weaver, still another central figure in the history of conservatism and perhaps best known for his book *Ideas Have Consequences*, opposed the atomic bombing of Japan and spoke with contempt of Theodore Roosevelt, who would "strut and bluster and intimidate our weaker neighbors." Weaver wrote an extraordinary essay on the immorality of total war in his book *Visions of Order*, arguing that "of the many things which cause us to feel that spirit indispensable to civilization has been weakened, none should arouse deeper alarm than total war."

The conservative sociologist Robert Nisbet reminded his audience that war was revolutionary, not conservative. He likewise warned that socialist proposals have often, under wartime conditions, become the law of the land.

These last three figures—Kirk, Weaver, and Nisbet—share something in common. One of the most useful and respected studies of American conservatism, George Nash's book *The Conservative Intellectual Movement in America Since 1945*, identifies these three men as the most important thinkers among what he calls traditionalist conservatives. That means the three most significant traditional conservative intellectuals in the postwar period were all wary of militarism to one degree or another. None were pacifists, naturally, but they all believed that war was something so materially and morally catastrophic that it genuinely had to be considered only a last resort. And since, as Randolph Bourne said, "war is the health of the state," they also understood the undesirable domestic side effects of war, such as taxes, debt, lost liberties, centralization, and the emasculation of the Constitution.

How does Israel, with which the United States has long enjoyed a special relationship, fit into this picture? I see no reason that our friendship with Israel cannot continue. I favor extending to Israel the same honest friendship that Jefferson and the Founding Fathers urged us to offer to all nations. But that also means no special privileges like foreign aid—a position I maintain vis-à-vis all other countries as well. That means I also favor discontinuing foreign aid to governments that are actual or potential enemies of Israel, which taken together receive much more American aid than Israel does. Giving aid to both sides has understandably made many average Israelis and American Jews conclude that the American government is hypocritically hedging its bets.

I oppose all foreign aid on principle, for reasons I detail in a later chapter. Foreign aid is not only immoral, since it involves the forced transfer of wealth, but it is also counterproductive, as a ceaseless stream of scholarship continues to show. Foreign aid has been a disaster in Africa, delaying sound economic reforms and encouraging wastefulness and statism. We should not wish it on our worst enemy, much less a friend. Moreover, since the aid has to be spent on products made by American corporations, it is really just a form of corporate welfare, which I can never support.

Only those with a very superficial attachment to Israel can really be happy that she continues to rely on over $2 billion in

American aid every year. In the absence of such grants, Israel would at last be under pressure to adopt a freer economy, thereby bringing about greater prosperity for her people and making it easier for her to be self-reliant. Foreign aid only inhibits salutary reforms like this, reforms that any true friend of Israel is eager to see. As a matter of fact, the Institute for Advanced Strategic and Political Studies in Jerusalem argues that "foreign aid is the greatest obstacle to economic freedom in Israel." It is an open secret that Israel's military industry is inefficient and top-heavy with bureaucracy, shortcomings that consistent American aid obviously encourages. Why make difficult adjustments when billions in aid can be counted on regardless of what you do?

Our government has also done Israel a disservice by effectively infringing on her sovereignty. Israel seeks American approval for military action she deems necessary, she consults with America on matters pertaining to her own borders, and she even seeks American approval for peace talks with her neighbors—approval that is not always forthcoming. This needs to stop. And with an arsenal of hundreds of nuclear weapons, Israel is more than capable of deterring or repelling any enemy. She should once again be in charge of her own destiny.

In the face of the human cost of war—the thousands of American servicemen killed, the tens of thousands wounded, the civilian deaths—a reckoning of its material costs may seem almost obtuse. But we are not speaking of a few billion dollars here and there. The costs of our foreign policy have become so great that they risk bringing the country to bankruptcy.

When I say "bankruptcy," I do not mean that the federal government will stop writing checks and spending money. The federal government is not likely to go out of business anytime soon. I mean that the checks and the money won't buy anything, because the dollar will have been destroyed.

Few Americans realize just how costly our foreign policy is. Larry Lindsey, senior economic adviser to the Bush administration, embarrassed the White House when he warned in the *Wall Street Journal* that the Iraq war could cost $100 to $200 billion. Outrageous, officials said. The course of events has made Lindsey's estimate into the epitome of optimism. In early 2006, Harvard's Linda Bilmes and Columbia's Joseph Stiglitz estimated the long-term costs of the war, including care for our maimed soldiers, at $2 trillion. By the end of the year they were saying that the $2 trillion figure was too low.

It isn't just the Iraq war that busts the budget—it's our overseas military presence as a whole. We have reached a point at which it now costs $1 trillion per year to maintain. One trillion dollars. The proposed Pentagon budget alone was $623 billion for 2008. "What's remarkable about this year's military budget," wrote one military analyst, "is that it's the largest budget since World War II, but, of course, we're not fighting World War II."

And just as in domestic spending, where higher budgets rarely translate into better performance, I am doubtful that much of this expenditure is actually contributing to our security. America would be much stronger and more secure if our government observed a noninterventionist foreign policy and put an end to its international overstretch. And that isn't just because foreign meddling makes us more enemies, though that commonsensical point is certainly correct. Beyond even that, we waste a staggering amount of manpower, hardware, and wealth on a bloated overseas presence that would be better devoted to protecting the United States itself. Our forces are stretched much too thin, what with our 700 bases around the world and all the nation-building work that conservatives not so long ago criticized Bill Clinton for imposing on our military.

We have had troops in Korea for over five and a half decades. We have had troops in Europe and Japan for about as long. How many years is enough? An American presence in these places was supposed to be temporary, persisting only during the military emergencies that were cited as justification for bringing them there. Milton Friedman was right: there is nothing so permanent as a "temporary" government program.

With a $9 trillion debt, perhaps $50 trillion in entitlement liabilities, and the dollar in free fall, how much longer can we afford this unnecessary and counterproductive extravagance?

While our government engages in deficit spending to fund its military exploits overseas, detracting from our own productivity, countries like China are filling the void by expanding their trade opportunities. I have never understood this talk of our military presence as a "strategic reserve of Western civilization." Instead, the best indication of our civilization has been our prestige in international trade. We should let the best measure of our American greatness come from free and peaceful trade with other nations, not from displays of our military might.

Now it would be a great step forward if we could even debate the foreign policy we have now, a policy that (with a few minor differences) is shared by the establishment of both major parties. One writer correctly labels it "the debate we never have." Although many Americans oppose the continued expansion of Big Government abroad, nonintervention is never presented to them as an option. The so-called debates between pundits they see on television or read in the newspaper carefully limit the range of debate to the point of insignificance. The debate is always framed in terms of which kind of interventionist strategy our government should pursue. The possibility that we should avoid bleeding ourselves dry in endless foreign meddling is not raised. For heaven's sake, what kind of debate is it in which all sides agree that America needs troops in 130 countries?

That may have been the kind of debate that the old *Pravda* once allowed, but where is the robust exchange of ideas that we should expect in a free society?

If we ever have such a debate, some Americans may conclude that the increased risk of terrorism is a price they are willing to pay in order to continue our government's interventionist foreign policy. Others will realize that foreign interventionism is bankrupting us and making us less secure. However it came out, at least we would have had the debate. At the end of such a debate, Michael Scheuer concludes, Americans "may decide that the foreign policy status quo that exists at the moment is what they want. But if they do, they will at least go into it with their eyes open, and know that they are in for an extended period of war, a tremendously bloody and costly war."

Meanwhile, our lack of debate has had terrible consequences for our republic. James Bamford observes that the leadership of al Qaeda hoped to lure us into a "desert Vietnam," an enormously expensive war that would deplete our resources and help their own recruitment by stirring up the locals against us. And that is just what happened. The war's ultimate cost is being estimated in the trillions. The dollar is collapsing. And more terrorists are being created. According to a study by the Global Research in International Affairs Center in Herzliya, Israel, the vast bulk of the foreign fighters in Iraq are people who had never been involved in terrorist activity before but have been radicalized by the U.S. presence in Iraq—the second holiest place in Islam.

The terrorists, in short, have played us like a fiddle. With the unnecessary and unprovoked attack on Iraq, our government gave them just what they wanted.

Americans have the right to defend themselves against attack; that is not at issue. But that is very different from launching a preemptive war against a country that had not attacked us and could not attack us, that lacked a navy and an air force, and whose military budget was a fraction of a percent of our own. A policy of overthrowing or destabilizing every regime our government dislikes is no strategy at all, unless our goal is international chaos and domestic impoverishment.

It is time for us to consider a strategic reassessment of our policy of foreign interventionism, occupation, and nation building. It is in our national interest to do so and in the interest of world peace. This is a message that resonates not only with the American people at large but also with U.S. military personnel: in the second quarter of 2007 our campaign raised more money from active duty and retired military than did any other Republican candidate, and in the third quarter we raised more than any candidate in either party. Then in the fourth quarter we received more money in military donations than all other Republicans put together. This message is popular, and it is based on American security, fiscal sanity, and common sense.

CHAPTER 3

The Constitution

Though written constitutions "may be violated in moments of passion or delusion," wrote Thomas Jefferson in 1802, "yet they furnish a text to which those who are watchful may again rally and recall the people."

Whether we are yet emerging from our own moment of disorientation after 9/11 is difficult to say. I believe, though, that enough Americans are taking a sober second look at what we have allowed our country to become, especially since that terrible day, that the Constitution may yet reemerge as a document to which the people may be rallied and recalled.

In early American history the Constitution figured heavily in political debate. People wanted to know, and politicians needed to justify, where the various schemes they debated in Congress were authorized in the Constitution. In the twenty-first century, by contrast, the Constitution is like the elephant at the tea party that everyone pretends not to notice.

The power of the executive branch, for instance, has expanded far beyond what the Framers of the Constitution envisioned.

One mechanism that has strengthened it is the executive order, an instrument by which presidents have exerted powers that our Constitution never intended them to have. An executive order is a command issued by the president that enjoys his authority alone, not having been passed by Congress. Executive orders can have legitimate functions. Presidents can carry out their constitutional duties or direct their subordinates by executive order, for instance. But they can also be a source of temptation for ambitious presidents (am I being redundant?), since they can always try to get away with using them as a substitute for formal legislation that they know they cannot get to pass. He can thereby circumvent the normal, constitutional legislative process.

Executive orders were rare in the nineteenth century; for a president to issue even several dozen was unusual. The first twentieth-century president to serve a full term, Theodore Roosevelt (who served two, in fact), issued over a thousand. His distant cousin Franklin Roosevelt issued over three thousand. Executive orders continue to serve as a potent weapon in the president's arsenal.

Congress has sometimes been complicit in presidential abuses of executive orders, either by giving express sanction to the president's action after the fact or ignoring the abuse of power altogether. This latter course is sometimes pursued when congressmen happen to favor the president's course of action but do not want to have to associate themselves with it (perhaps because it is controversial or politically sensitive). With executive orders, presidents can commit our troops to undeclared wars, destroy industries, or make unprecedented social-policy changes. And they remain unaccountable because often these actions occur behind the door of the Oval Office, are distributed without notice, and then executed in stealth. This is a travesty against our constitutional system, and any president worthy of the office would absolutely forswear the use of executive orders except when he can show express constitutional or statutory authority for his action.

Yet another abuse, though, and all the more troubling for being unknown to most Americans, involves the use of something called presidential signing statements. When the president signs a bill into law, he sometimes accompanies the signing with a statement, not necessarily read aloud at the signing ceremony but inserted into the record all the same. This practice was not unheard of in previous administrations, though it was nearly always employed for ceremonial purposes: to thank supporters, to point out the significance of the legislation, and in pursuit of rhetorical ends of a similar kind.

The Bush administration, on the other hand, has very often used the signing statement as a vehicle either for expressing the manner in which the president intends to interpret certain provisions of a law (his interpretation being frequently at odds with the one Congress obviously intended), or even for making clear his intention of not enforcing the provision in question at all. It is not always easy to determine whether the president has followed through on these threats, since they are so often made in areas that the White House shrouds in secrecy: foreign policy and privacy violations. In 2005, though, the Government Accountability Office gave us a very rough estimate of how many of these threatened refusals to enforce legislative provisions were followed up on: in about one-third of the nineteen cases it examined, the provision was not being enforced. Law professor Jonathan Turley was blunt: "By using signing statements to this extent, the president becomes a government unto himself."

The Bush administration has challenged more legislative provisions in this way than any other presidential administration in American history. If Bill Clinton had done this, we would still be hearing about it. Today, few Republicans in public life have been courageous or principled enough to speak out against a clear abuse of power. (Among them are Bruce Fein, associate deputy attorney general under Ronald Reagan, and former Congressman Bob Barr.)

Again, an American president must pledge never to use the signing statement as an alternative, unconstitutional form of legislative power, and Congress and the American people should hold him to it.

———

Much of the recent revival of interest in the Constitution centers around the Bill of Rights and the war on terror, a subject I discuss elsewhere in this book. I could not be more sympathetic to these concerns. However, Americans must remember that the Constitution was designed not merely to prevent the federal government from violating the rights that later appeared in the Bill of Rights. It was also intended to limit the federal government's overall scope. Article I, Section 8, lists the powers of Congress. Common law held such lists of powers to be exhaustive.

According to the Tenth Amendment to the Constitution, all powers not delegated to the federal government by the states (in Article I, Section 8) and not prohibited to the states in the Constitution (in Article I, Section 10) are reserved to the states or to the people. Thomas Jefferson held that this principle formed the very foundation of our Constitution. It was a guarantee that the experience Americans endured under the British would not be repeated, and that political decisions would be made by their own local legislatures rather than by a distant central government that would be much more difficult, if not impossible, for them to control.

Jefferson's approach to the Constitution—which he adamantly believed could be understood by the average person and was not some secret teaching that had to be divined by immortals in black robes—was refreshingly simple. If a proposed federal law was not listed among the powers granted to Congress in Article I, Section 8, then no matter how otherwise attractive it seemed, it had to be rejected on constitutional grounds. If it were especially wise or desirable, there would be no difficulty in amending the Constitution to allow for it. And according to Jefferson we should always bear in mind, to the extent possible, the original intention of those who drafted and ratified the Constitution: "On every question of construction, carry ourselves back to the time when the Constitution was adopted, recollect the spirit manifested in the debates, and instead of trying what meaning may be squeezed out of the text, or invented against it, conform to the probable one in which it was passed."

"Our peculiar security is in possession of a written Constitution," Jefferson advised us. "Let us not make it a blank paper by construction." Jefferson was afraid, in other words, that we would allow our government to interpret the Constitution so broadly that we may as well be governed by a blank piece of paper. The limitations the Constitution placed on the federal government had to be taken seriously if we expected to maintain a free society. There would always be a powerful temptation to allow the federal government to do something many people wanted, but that the

Constitution did not authorize. Since the amendment process is time-consuming, there would be a further temptation: just exercise the unauthorized power without amending the Constitution. But then what is the point of having a Constitution at all?

It is true that although Jefferson was a great constitutional exegete, he was not himself present at the Constitutional Convention. But Jefferson's ideas were not his alone: they reflected many of the sentiments expressed at his state's ratifying convention by such important and diverse figures as Edmund Randolph, George Nicholas, and Patrick Henry—not to mention John Taylor of Caroline, perhaps the most prolific political pamphleteer of the 1790s. Jefferson was merely giving voice to this much larger tradition when he expounded his strict-constructionist views.

"Confidence is everywhere the parent of despotism," said Jefferson in 1798. "Free government is founded in jealousy, and not in confidence. . . . In matters of Power, let no more be heard of confidence in man, but bind him down from mischief by the chains of the Constitution." Nearly a quarter of a century later, Jefferson could still be heard uttering the same warning: "Is confidence or discretion, or is STRICT LIMIT, the principle of our Constitution?"

I sometimes hear the objection that certain phrases in the Constitution give the federal government more power than what is listed in Article I, Section 8. The "general welfare" clause is often cited, although equally dishonest interpretations of the interstate commerce and "necessary and proper" clauses have also been put forward. I have already noted that common law held lists of powers such as the one in Article I, Section 8, to be exhaustive, a point that refutes the idea that qualifying phrases like "general welfare" could give an open-ended character to the powers themselves. But the testimony of the Framers is also very clear. James Madison wrote, "If Congress can do whatever in their discretion can be done by money, and will promote the General Welfare, the Government is no longer a limited one, possessing enumerated powers, but an indefinite one, subject to particular exceptions." Toward the end of his life, he added: "With respect to the words general welfare, I have always regarded them as qualified by the detail of powers connected with them. To take them in a literal and unlimited sense would be a metamorphosis of the Constitution into a character which there is a host of proofs was not contemplated by its creators." And of course, as Madison elsewhere wrote, if the federal government really had been intended to carry out whatever action might promote the general welfare, what was the point of listing its specific powers in Article I, Section 8, since this superpower would have covered all of those anyway?

The typical reply to this argument, if one is forthcoming at all, is that Alexander Hamilton had a different view of the "general welfare" clause. Indeed he did, but what does that prove? Hamilton was dramatically out of step with most of the other delegates to the Constitutional Convention. He was also inconsistent in his views, saying one thing before the Constitution was ratified and another after ratification. In his 1791 Report on Manufactures, he denied that the spending authority of Congress was confined to the powers enumerated in Article I, Section 8, laying out a broad array of areas he wanted to see receive government funding—precisely the areas he denied the national government would have jurisdiction over when he wrote Federalist No. 17 and Federalist No. 34 several years earlier.

Patrick Henry raised precisely this concern as the ratification of the Constitution was being debated in Virginia: wasn't "general welfare" a dangerously open-ended phrase that would permit the federal government to do whatever it wanted, since government officials could blandly claim that all its measures were intended to promote the general welfare? Supporters of the Constitution gave Henry a definitive answer: no, "general welfare" did not and could not have such a broad meaning.

Now, isn't our Constitution a "living" document that evolves in accordance with experience and changing times, as we're so often told? No—a thousand times no. If we feel the need to change our Constitution, we are free to amend it. In 1817, James Madison reminded Congress that the Framers had "marked out in the [Constitution] itself a safe and practicable mode of improving it as experience might suggest"—a reference to the amendment process. But that is not what advocates of a so-called living Constitution have in mind. They favor a system in which the federal government, and in particular the federal courts, are at liberty—even in the absence of any amendment—to interpret the Constitution altogether differently from how it was understood by those who drafted it and those who voted to ratify it.

Leave aside the alleged problem of determining exactly what the Framers intended by this or that constitutional clause— supporters of the living Constitution must be able to figure out the original intent well enough if they are so sure we need to evolve away from it. If the people agreed to a particular understanding of the Constitution, and over the course of the intervening years they have performed no official act (such as amending the Constitution in accordance with their evolved ideas) reversing that original understanding, by what right may government unilaterally change the terms of its contract with the people, interpreting its words to mean something very different from what the American people had all along been told they meant?

A "living" Constitution is just the thing any government would be delighted to have, for whenever the people complain that their Constitution has been violated, the government can trot out its judges to inform the people that they've simply misunderstood: the Constitution, you see, has merely evolved with the times. Thus, as in Orwell's *Animal Farm*, "no animal shall sleep in a bed" becomes "no animal shall sleep in a bed with sheets," "no animal shall drink alcohol" becomes "no animal shall drink alcohol to excess," and "no animal shall kill any other animal" becomes "no animal shall kill any other animal without cause."

That's why on this issue I agree with historian Kevin Gutzman, who says that those who would give us a "living" Constitution are actually giving us a dead Constitution, since such a thing is completely unable to protect us against the encroachments of government power.

During my public life I have earned the nickname Dr. No, a reference to my previous occupation as a physician combined with my willingness to stand against the entire Congress if necessary to vote no on some proposed measure. (I am told I have been the sole "no" vote in Congress more often than all other members of Congress put together.) As a matter of fact, I don't especially care for this nickname, since it may give people the impression that I am a contrarian for its own sake, and that for some reason I simply relish saying no. In those no votes, as in all my congressional votes,

I have thought of myself as saying yes to the Constitution and to freedom.

———

The Constitution has much to say to us regarding foreign policy, if we will only listen. For over half a century the two major parties have done their best to ignore what it has to say, especially when it comes to the initiation of hostilities. Both parties have allowed the president to exercise powers of which the Framers of the Constitution thought they had deprived him. And since both parties have been contemptuous of the Constitution's allocation of war powers between the president and Congress, neither one—with very rare exceptions—ever calls the other out on it.

The Framers did not want the American president to resemble the British king, from whom they had separated just a few years earlier. Even Alexander Hamilton, who was known to be sympathetic toward the British model, was at pains in the *Federalist Papers* to point out a critical difference between the king and the president as envisioned by the Constitution:

> The President is to be commander-in-chief of the army and navy of the United States. In this respect his authority would be nominally the same with that of the king of Great Britain, but in substance much inferior to it. It would amount to nothing more than the supreme command and direction of the military and naval forces, as first General and admiral of the Confederacy; while that of the British king extends to the *declaring* of war and to the *raising* and *regulating* of fleets and armies—all of which, by the

Constitution under consideration, would appertain to the legislature.

Whatever kind of evidence you want to examine, whether constitutional or historical, the verdict is clear: Congress was supposed to declare war, and the president in turn was to direct the war once it was declared. This rule was scrupulously observed throughout American history until 1950 and the Korean War. Short of a full-fledged declaration of war, in lesser conflicts Congress nevertheless authorized hostilities by statute. Any exceptions to this general rule involved military activities so minor and on such a small scale as hardly to be worth mentioning.

The Korean War was the great watershed in the modern presidential power grab in war-making. President Harry Truman sent Americans halfway around the world without so much as a nod in the direction of Congress. According to Truman, authorization from the United Nations to use force was quite sufficient, and rendered congressional consent unnecessary. (Apart from being dangerous, that idea is simply false: Article 43 of the United Nations Charter states that any United Nations authorization to use force must be subsequently referred to the governments of each nation "in accordance with their respective constitutional processes"; this principle was reaffirmed in the United States in the debates over the United Nations Participation Act of 1945.) Truman also claimed that the Constitution's commander-in-chief clause gave him the authority to plunge America into war on his own initiative.

Truman's interpretation of the Constitution was completely untenable. Nothing in American history supports it: not the Constitutional Convention, the state ratifying conventions, the

Federalist Papers, early Court decisions, or the actual practice of war-making throughout most of American history. Even the early examples that are typically cited as evidence of presidential war-making—John Adams's actions during the Quasi War with France, and Thomas Jefferson's confrontation with the Barbary pirates of north Africa—show no such thing. Both of these minor incidents were carried out according to congressional statute, with the Supreme Court ruling that a presidential directive contrary to such statutes was of no force.

In spite of its complete lack of constitutional foundation, this belief that the president may take the country to war on his own authority, without consulting anyone, has become the conventional wisdom in both major parties, although there has been a modest backlash against it since the Iraq war. Neoconservatives have been particularly eager to promote this deviation from the Constitution. This, it seems, is their version of the "living" Constitution.

Interestingly enough, one of the chief critics of Truman's exercise of power was Senator Robert A. Taft, one of the most conservative Republicans of his day (and who was in fact known as "Mr. Republican"). Speaking on the Senate floor, Taft denounced Truman's arguments and behavior in no uncertain terms:

> I desire this afternoon to discuss only the question of the power claimed by the President to send troops anywhere in the world and involve us in any war in the world and involve us in any war in which he chooses to involve us. I wish to assert the powers of Congress, and to point out that Congress has the power to prevent any such action by the President; that he has no such power under the Con-

stitution; and that it is incumbent upon the Congress to assert clearly its own constitutional powers unless it desires to lose them.

"In the long run," Taft went on,

the question we must decide involves vitally, I think, not only the freedom of the people of the United States, but the peace of the people of the United States. . . . If in the great field of foreign policy the President has arbitrary and unlimited power, as he now claims, then there is an end to freedom in the United States in a great realm of domestic activity which affects, in the long run, every person in the United States. . . . If the President has unlimited power to involve us in war, war is more likely. History shows that . . . arbitrary rulers are more inclined to favor war than are the people, at any time.

Responding to various defenses offered by the president and administration officials, Taft declared: "I deny the conclusions of the documents presented by the President or by the executive department, and I would say that if the doctrines therein proclaimed prevailed, they would bring an end to government by the people, because our foreign interests are going gradually to predominate and require a larger and larger place in the field of the activities of our people."

In 2002, as war with Iraq loomed, I proposed that Congress officially declare war against Iraq, making clear that I intended to oppose my own measure. The point was to underscore our constitutional responsibility to declare war before commencing major military operations, rather than leaving the decision to the president or passing resolutions that delegate to the president the decision-making power over war. The chairman of the International Relations Committee responded by saying, "There are things in the Constitution that have been overtaken by events, by time. Declaration of war is one of them. There are things no longer relevant to a modern society. We are saying to the president, use your judgment. [What you have proposed is] inappropriate, anachronistic; it isn't done any more."

What a relief that we have people in our government who will keep us posted on which constitutional provisions they have decided are no longer "relevant"!

Now, didn't Congress authorize the war in Iraq after all? No, and certainly not in a manner consistent with the Constitution. Congress has no constitutional authority to delegate to the president the decision regarding whether to use military force. That power was consciously and for good reason put in the hands of the people's elected representatives in the legislature.

Louis Fisher, one of the nation's experts on the subject of presidential war powers, described what happened this way: "The resolution helped bring pressure on the Security Council to send inspectors into Iraq to search for weapons of mass destruction. They found nothing. As to whether war should or should not occur, the committee washed its hands. By passing legislation that allowed the president to make that decision, Congress transferred a primary constitutional duty from the legislative branch to the executive branch. That is precisely what the Framers fought against."

Meanwhile, all these wars have to be fought by someone, and that is why the military draft is being spoken about more and more. Given the overseas ambitions of so much of our political class, a return of the draft may actually be closer than we realize. (As a matter of fact we have something like a de facto draft already, what with all the extensions being imposed on our troops.) Having stretched our military to the breaking point, where do they expect to find the troops for the next conflict?

The draft is a totalitarian institution that is based on the idea that the government owns you and can dispose of your life as it wishes. Republican Senator Robert Taft said that the draft was "far more typical of totalitarian nations than of democratic nations. It is absolutely opposed to the principles of individual liberty, which have always been considered a part of American democracy." Conservative thinker Russell Kirk referred to the draft as "slavery." Military conscription, said Ronald Reagan in 1979, "rests on the assumption that your kids belong to the state. . . . That assumption isn't a new one. The Nazis thought it was a great idea." The following year, in a speech at Louisiana State University, Reagan added:

> I oppose registration for the draft . . . because I believe the security of freedom can best be achieved by security through freedom. The all-voluntary force is based on the sound and historic American principle of voluntary commitment to defense of freedom. . . . The United States of America believes a free people do not have to be coerced in defending their country or their values and that the principle of freedom is the best and only foundation upon which a defense of freedom can be made. My vision of a secure America is based on my belief that freedom calls forth the best in the human spirit and that the defense of freedom can and will

best be made out of love of country, a love that needs no coercion. Out of such a love, a real security will develop, because in the final analysis, the free human heart and spirit are the best and most reliable defense.

In late 1814, fearing that conscription was about to come to America, Daniel Webster delivered a stirring speech against it on the House floor. (Webster served for many years in both the House and the Senate, and he held the office of secretary of state in both the early 1840s and early 1850s.) Webster's belief in a strong central government made his words against the draft all the more striking. "Where is it written in the Constitution," he demanded, "in what article or section is it contained, that you may take children from their parents, and parents from their children, and compel them to fight the battles of any war, in which the folly or the wickedness of Government may engage it?" The draft was irreconcilable with both the principles of a free society and the provisions of the Constitution. "In granting Congress the power to raise armies," Webster explained, "the people have granted all the means which are ordinary and usual, and which are consistent with the liberties and security of the people themselves, and they have granted no others. . . . A free government with arbitrary means to administer it is a contradiction; a free government without adequate provisions for personal security is an absurdity; a free government, with an uncontrolled power of military conscription, is a solecism, at once the most ridiculous and abominable that ever entered into the head of man."

Webster was right both morally and constitutionally. Nowhere in the Constitution is the federal government given the power to conscript citizens. The power to raise armies is not a power to force people into the army. As Webster put it,

> I almost disdain to go to quotations and references to prove that such an abominable doctrine has no foundation in the Constitution of the country. It is enough to know that that instrument was intended as the basis of a free government, and that the power contended for is incompatible with any notion of personal liberty. An attempt to maintain this doctrine upon the provisions of the Constitution is an exercise of perverse ingenuity to extract slavery from substance of a free government.

He continued:

> Congress having, by the Constitution, a power to raise armies, the Secretary [of War] contends that no restraint is to be imposed on the exercise of this power, except such as is expressly stated in the written letter of the instrument. In other words, that Congress may execute its powers, by any means it chooses, unless such means are particularly prohibited. But the general nature and object of the Constitution impose as rigid a restriction on the means of exercising power as could be done by the most explicit injunctions. It is the first principle applicable to such a case, that no construction shall be admitted which impairs the general nature and character of the instrument. A free constitution of government is to be construed upon free principles, and every branch of its provisions is to receive such an interpretation as is full of its general spirit. No means are to be

taken by implication which would strike us absurdly if expressed. And what would have been more absurd than for this Constitution to have said that to secure the great blessings of liberty it gave to government uncontrolled power of military conscription? Yet such is the absurdity which it is made to exhibit, under the commentary of the Secretary of War.

Lesser forms of the draft, such as compulsory "national service," are based on the same unacceptable premise. Young people are not raw material to be employed by the political class on behalf of whatever fashionable political, military, or social cause catches its fancy. In a free society, their lives are not the playthings of government.

One of the most contentious issues in our public life over the past three and a half decades has been abortion. As a physician, and in particular as an obstetrician who has delivered over 4,000 babies, I have always had a special interest in the subject of abortion. When I studied medicine at Duke Medical School from 1957 to 1961, the subject was never raised. By the time of my medical residency at the University of Pittsburgh in the mid-1960s, though, wholesale defiance of the laws against abortion was taking place in various parts of the country, including my own.

Residents were encouraged to visit various operating rooms in order to observe the procedures that were being done. One day I walked into an operating room without knowing what I was walking into, and the doctors were in the middle of performing a C-section. It was actually an abortion by hysterotomy. The woman was probably six months along in her pregnancy, and the child she was carrying weighed over two pounds. At that time doctors were not especially sophisticated, for lack of a better term, when it came to killing the baby prior to delivery, so they went ahead with delivery and put the baby in a bucket in the corner of the room. The baby tried to breathe, and tried to cry, and everyone in the room pretended the baby wasn't there. I was deeply shaken by this experience, and it hit me at that moment just how important the life issue was.

I have heard the arguments in favor of abortion many times, and they have always disturbed me deeply. A popular academic argument for abortion demands that we think of the child in the womb as a "parasite" that the woman has the right to expel from her body. But the same argument justifies outright infanticide, since it applies just as well to an infant *outside* the womb: newborns require even more attention and care, and in that sense are even more "parasitic."

If we can be so callous as to refer to a growing child in a mother's womb as a parasite, I fear for our country's future all the more. Whether it is war or abortion, we conceal the reality of violent acts through linguistic contrivances meant to devalue human lives we find inconvenient. Dead civilians become "collateral damage," are ignored altogether, or are rationalized away on the Leninist grounds that to make an omelet you have to break some eggs. (The apostle Paul, on the other hand, condemned the idea that we should do evil that good may come.) People ask an expectant mother how her baby is doing. They do not ask how her fetus is doing, or her blob of tissue, or her parasite. But that is what her baby becomes as soon as the child is declared to be unwanted. In both cases, we try to make human life into something less than human, simply according to our will.

When *Roe v. Wade* was decided in 1973, striking down abortion laws all over the country, even some supporters of abortion were embarrassed by the decision as a matter of constitutional law. John Hart Ely, for instance, wrote in the *Yale Law Review*: "What is frightening about *Roe* is that this super-protected right is not inferable from the language of the Constitution, the framers' thinking respecting the specific problem in issue, any general value derivable from the provisions they included, or the nation's governmental structure." The decision, he said, "is not constitutional law and gives almost no sense of an obligation to try to be."

The federal government should not play any role in the abortion issue, according to the Constitution. Apart from waiting forever for Supreme Court justices who will rule in accordance with the Constitution, however, Americans who care about our fundamental law and/or are concerned about abortion do have some legislative recourse. Article III, Section 2, of the Constitution gives Congress the power to strip the federal courts, including the Supreme Court, of jurisdiction over broad categories of cases. In the wake of the 1857 *Dred Scott* decision, abolitionists spoke of depriving the courts of jurisdiction in cases dealing with slavery. The courts were stripped of authority over Reconstruction policy in the late 1860s.

If the federal courts refuse to abide by the Constitution, the Congress should employ this constitutional remedy. By a simple majority, Congress could strip the federal courts of jurisdiction over abortion, thereby overturning the obviously unconstitutional *Roe*. At that point, the issue would revert to the states, where it constitutionally belongs, since no appeal to federal courts on the matter could be heard. (I have proposed exactly this in H.R. 300.)

Let us remember, though, that the law can do only so much. The law isn't what allowed abortion; abortions were already being done in the 1960s against the law. The courts came along and conformed to the social and moral changes that were taking place in society. Law reflects the morality of the people. Ultimately, law or no law, it is going to be up to us as parents, as clergy, and as citizens—in the way we raise our children, how we interact and talk with our friends and neighbors, and the good example we give—to bring about changes to our culture toward greater respect for life.

To those who argue that we cannot allow the states to make decisions on abortion since some will make the wrong ones, I reply that that is an excellent argument for world government— for how can we allow individual *countries* to decide on abortion or other moral issues, if some may make the wrong decisions? Yet the dangers of a world government surely speak for themselves.

Let us therefore adopt the constitutional position, one that is achievable and can yield good results but that shuns the utopian idea that all evil can be eradicated. The Founding Fathers' approach will not solve all problems, and it will not be perfect. But anyone expecting perfection in this world is going to be consistently disappointed.

The same holds true for issues like prayer in schools. Such issues were never meant to be decided by federal judges. The whole point of the American Revolution was to vindicate the principle of local self-government. The British had denied that the colonial legislatures were exclusively endowed with the power to make political decisions for their peoples. The colonists, on the other hand, insisted that they would be governed only by their elected representatives. That remained the operative principle in the Articles of Confederation as well as the Constitution: local legislatures are presumed to hold authority except in areas in which they have expressly given up that authority.

We have come to consider it normal for nine judges in Washington to decide on social policies that affect every neighborhood, family, and individual in America. One side of the debate hopes the nine will impose one set of values, and the other side favors a different set. The underlying premise—that this kind of monolith is desirable, or that no alternative is possible—is never examined, or at least not nearly as often as it should be. The Founding Fathers did not intend for every American neighborhood to be exactly the same—a totalitarian impulse if there ever was one—or that disputes over competing values should be decided by federal judges. This is the constitutional approach to deciding all issues that are not spelled out explicitly in our founding document: let neighbors and localities govern themselves.

The Founding Fathers would be astonished to observe how politicized our society has become, with every matter on which people differ becoming a federal issue to be resolved in Washington. Jefferson warned, "When all government, domestic and foreign, in little as in great things, shall be drawn to Washington as the center of all power, it will render powerless the checks provided of one government on another, and will become as venal and oppressive as the government from which we separated." Are we listening?

In short, just as we should reject empire abroad, we should also reject it at home. One-size-fits-all social policy, dictated by unelected judges from an imperial capital, is not the system Americans signed on for when they ratified the Constitution, and they have never formally sanctioned such a thing.

Some people claim that the doctrine of states' rights, one of Thomas Jefferson's central principles, has been responsible for racism. But racism, a disorder of the heart, can become entrenched in any political environment, whether highly centralized like Hitler's Germany or highly decentralized like our own country. In *Mein Kampf,* Hitler spoke with delight of the process by which governments around the world were becoming more centralized, with states and local governments having less and less power. It was a trend he wanted to see continue in Germany, in order to build "a powerful national Reich" in which the central government could impose its will without having to worry about recalcitrant states. Hitler wrote:

> National Socialism as a matter of principle, must lay claim to the right to force its principles on the whole German nation without consideration of previous federated state boundaries, and to educate in its ideas and conceptions. Just as the churches do not feel bound and limited by political boundaries, no more does the National Socialist idea feel limited by the individual state territories of our fatherland. The National Socialist doctrine is not the servant of individual federated states, but shall some day become the master of the German nation.

No form of political organization, therefore, is immune to cruel abuses like the Jim Crow laws, whereby government sets out to legislate on how groups of human beings are allowed to interact with one another. Peaceful civil disobedience to unjust laws, which I support with every fiber of my being, can sometimes be necessary at any level of government. It falls upon the people, in the last resort, to stand against injustice no matter where it occurs.

In the long run, the only way racism can be overcome is through the philosophy of individualism, which I have promoted throughout my life. Our rights come to us not because we belong to some group, but our rights come to us as individuals. And it is as individuals that we should judge one another. Racism is a particularly odious form of collectivism whereby individuals are treated not on their merits but on the basis of group identity. Nothing in my political philosophy, which is the exact opposite of the racial totalitarianism of the twentieth century, gives aid or comfort to such thinking. To the contrary, my philosophy of individualism is the most radical intellectual challenge to racism ever posed.

Government exacerbates racial thinking and undermines individualism because its very existence encourages people to organize along racial lines in order to lobby for benefits for their group. That lobbying, in turn, creates animosity and suspicion among all groups, each of which believes that it is getting less of its fair share than the others.

Instead, we should quit thinking in terms of race—yes, in 2008 it is still necessary to say that we should stop thinking in terms of race—and recognize that freedom and prosperity benefit all Americans. As Thomas Sowell points out, lobbyists for various racial groups will spend all their time trying to enact programs that specifically help their own group, even though that group would reap far more benefit from advancing economic freedom in general. He gives the example of taxi licensing restrictions, a government policy that disproportionately hurts blacks. But since it is not thought of as a racial issue per se, racial pressure groups do absolutely nothing to overturn it. That's another reason we should stop thinking in terms of race. Consider Sowell:

Politically, however, it makes far more sense for a black leader to fight tooth and nail for a hundred more CETA [Comprehensive Employment and Training Act] jobs in the Philadelphia ghetto than to fight for an end to taxi licensing restrictions, even though the latter would probably mean thousands more jobs for blacks—jobs with far higher pay than CETA jobs and of permanent duration. Ghetto jobs are an earmarked benefit, however few, tenuous and low paid. *Benefits to blacks as members of the general public are no feather in a black leader's cap, even if blacks are benefited more than others by gaining access that was nearly impossible for them before* [emphasis added].

As I discuss in Chapter 5, the federal war on drugs has wrought disproportionate harm on minority communities. Allowing for states' rights here would surely be an improvement, for the states could certainly do a better and more sensible job than the federal government has been doing if they were free to decide the issue for themselves. And although people studying my record will discover how consistent I have been over the years, they will uncover one major shift: in recent years I have dropped my support for the federal death penalty. It is a dangerous power for the federal government to have, and it is exercised in a discriminatory way: if you are poor and black, you are much more likely to receive this punishment.

We should not think in terms of whites, blacks, Hispanics, and other such groups. That kind of thinking only divides us. The only us-versus-them thinking in which we might indulge is the people—*all* the people—versus the government, which loots and lies to us all, threatens our liberties, and shreds our Constitution. That's not a white or black issue. That's an American issue, and it's one on which Americans of all races can unite in a spirit of goodwill. That may be why polls in 2007 found ours the most popular Republican campaign among black voters.

———

If our government were scrupulously faithful to the Constitution, we would not need to be especially concerned when a person who represents a philosophy different from our own takes political office. Our Constitution delegates relatively few tasks to the federal government, so it should almost be a matter of indifference who is elected. We wouldn't have to worry that a social policy of which we disapproved would be imposed on our neighborhood at the whim of the new president and his court appointees, or that more of our money would be stolen to fund yet another government boondoggle. And we would also be spared the spectacle of countless American individuals and corporations frantically donating to candidates for political office during election years in order to reserve a place on the federal gravy train if their favorite should win.

I've often cautioned conservatives who are tempted to give more power to the federal government in general or the executive branch in particular that those additional powers will be available to whoever takes office next—and that person may not be to your liking. I now find myself offering the same words of caution to liberals: whatever temptation you may have to exceed the powers granted under the Constitution, understand that you are opening a Pandora's box. Once we lose our respect for the Constitution and begin interpreting it so that it happens to permit our pet programs, we have no right to be surprised when our political opponents come along with their own ideas for interpreting the Constitution loosely.

To be sure, the U.S. Constitution is not perfect. Few human contrivances are. But it is a pretty good one, I think, and it defines and limits the scope of government. When we get into the habit of disregarding it or—what is the same thing—interpreting certain key phrases so broadly as to allow the federal government to do whatever it wants, we do so at our peril. We will wind up with a situation like the one we face right now, that few Americans are happy with.

I do not believe that most Americans want to continue down this path: undeclared wars without end, more and more police-state measures, and a Constitution that may as well not exist. But this is not a fated existence. We do not have to live in this kind of America. It is not too late to rally and recall our people to the Constitution, the rule of law, and our traditional American republic.

CHAPTER 4

Economic Freedom

E conomic freedom is based on a simple moral rule: everyone has a right to his or her life and property, and no one has the right to deprive anyone of these things.

To some extent, everyone accepts this principle. For instance, anyone going to his neighbor's home and taking his money at gunpoint, regardless of all the wonderful, selfless things he promised to do with it, would be promptly arrested as a thief.

But for some reason it is considered morally acceptable when government does that very thing. We have allowed government to operate according to its own set of moral rules. Frédéric Bastiat, one of the great political and economic writers of all time, called this "legal plunder."

Bastiat identified three approaches we could take to such plunder:

1. The few plunder the many.
2. Everybody plunders everybody.
3. Nobody plunders anybody.

We presently follow option number two: everyone seeks to use government to enrich himself at his neighbor's expense. That's why Bastiat called the state "the great fiction through which everybody endeavors to live at the expense of everybody else."

Now here's a radical idea: what if we pursued option number three and decided to stop robbing one another? What if we decided that there was a better, more humane way for people to interact with each other? What if we stopped doing things we would consider morally outrageous if done by private individuals but that we consider perfectly all right when carried out by government in the name of "public policy"?

By "legal plunder" Bastiat meant any use of government that enriched one group of people at the expense of another, and which would be illegal if private individuals tried to carry it out themselves. He was not speaking only or even primarily about programs that are supposed to help the poor. Bastiat was a keen enough observer of the human condition to realize that people of all classes are happy to use the machinery of state, if they can get away with it, to benefit themselves instead of earning their way in the world honestly.

The rich are more than happy to secure for themselves a share of the loot—for example, in the form of subsidized low-interest loans (as with the Export-Import Bank), bailouts when their risky loans go sour, or regulatory schemes that hurt their smaller competitors or make it harder for new ones to enter an industry. Of course, industry leaders will portray such regulation as being for the public good, and media outlets, inclined to give all regulation the benefit of the doubt, will do their best to make sure Americans buy it.

This simple idea, that government should stay out of the looting business and leave people to their own pursuits, has had great moral appeal throughout U.S. history. The American poet Walt Whitman urged that "no man's benefit [be] achieved at the expense of his neighbors. . . . While mere politicians, in their narrow minds, are sweating and fuming with their complicated statutes, this one single rule . . . is enough to form the starting point of all that is necessary in government; to make no more laws than those useful for preventing a man or body of men from infringing on the rights of other men."

Likewise, William Leggett, a Jacksonian editorial writer, believed that government should be restricted to "the making of *general laws*, uniform and universal in their operation," for the sole purpose of protecting people and their property.

> Governments have no right to interfere with the pursuits of individuals, as guaranteed by those general laws, by offering encouragements and granting privileges to any particular class of industry, or any select bodies of men, inasmuch as all classes of industry and all men are equally important to the general welfare, and equally entitled to protection.
>
> Whenever a Government assumes the power of discriminating between the different classes of the community, it becomes, in effect, the arbiter of their prosperity, and exercises a power not contemplated by any intelligent people in delegating their sovereignty to their rulers. It then becomes the great regulator of the profits of every species of industry, and reduces men from a dependence on their own exertions, to a dependence on the caprices of their Government. Governments possess no delegated right to tamper with individual industry a single hair's-

breadth beyond what is essential to protect the rights of person and property.

In the exercise of this power of intermeddling with the private pursuits and individual occupations of the citizen, a Government may at pleasure elevate one class and depress another; it may one day legislate exclusively for the farmer, the next for the mechanic, and the third for the manufacturer, who all thus become the mere puppets of legislative cobbling and tinkering, instead of independent citizens, relying on their own resources for their prosperity. It assumes the functions which belong alone to an overruling Providence, and affects to become the universal dispenser of good and evil.

Consider a single, almost trivial example of government favoritism: sugar quotas. The United States government limits the amount of sugar that can be imported from around the world. These quotas make sugar more expensive for all Americans, since they now have fewer choices as a result of diminished competition. The quotas also put at a competitive disadvantage all those businesses that use sugar to produce their own products. That's one reason that American colas use corn syrup instead of sugar: American sugar, thanks to the quotas, is simply too expensive. (And it's also a reason that colas in other countries taste so much better.)

The number of people who work in the American sugar industry is of course very small when compared to the American population as a whole. How, then, did they manage to get a government policy enacted that harms the vast bulk of their fellow citizens? The answer is that the benefits are concentrated while the costs are dispersed. The small number of people who work in the sugar industry benefit substantially from the quota. It makes sense for the sugar industry to employ professional lobbyists first to get and then to continue this concentrated flow of benefits.

On the other hand, since the costs of these policies are spread out across the entire American people, the cost to any one purchaser of sugar or products containing sugar is very minor. It makes no sense for the general public to marshal resources to lobby for the repeal of the program; it is hardly worth their time even to be informed about it. Each consumer might pay an extra fifty to one hundred dollars per year thanks to the program—a pittance compared to what industry earns from it, and not nearly enough to make it worthwhile to hire lobbyists or launch any serious effort to abolish it. And so the tendency is for this fleecing of the public to get worse and worse: the concentrated benefits it brings are too hard to resist, but the dispersed costs are too small to justify any effort against it.

Multiply this modest example by about a million, to account for the countless other predatory schemes that special interests have imposed on our economy, and you have some idea of the impact of legal plunder.

If we believe in liberty, we must also remember what William Graham Sumner called "the forgotten man." The forgotten man is the one whose labor is exploited in order to benefit whatever political cause catches the government's fancy.

The type and formula of most schemes of philanthropy or humanitarianism is this: A and B put their heads together to decide what C shall be made to do for D. The radical vice of all these schemes, from a sociological point of view, is that C is not allowed a voice in the matter, and his position, character, and interests, as well as the ultimate effects on society through C's interests, are entirely overlooked. I call C the Forgotten Man. . . .

They therefore ignore entirely the source from which they must draw all the energy which they employ in their remedies, and they ignore all the effects on other members of society than the ones they have in view. They are always under the dominion of the superstition of government, and, forgetting that a government produces nothing at all, they leave out of sight the first fact to be remembered in all social discussion—that the state cannot get a cent for any man without taking it from some other man, and this latter must be a man who has produced and saved it. This latter is the Forgotten Man.

Once government does become involved in something, intellectual and institutional inertia tends to keep it there for good. People lose their political imagination. It becomes impossible to conceive of dealing with the matter in any other way. Repealing the new bureaucracy becomes unthinkable. Mythology about how terrible things were in the old days becomes the conventional wisdom. Meanwhile, the bureaucracy itself, with a vested interest in maintaining itself and increasing its funding, employs all the resources it can to ensuring that it gets a bigger budget next year, regardless of its performance. In fact, the worse it does, the more funding it is likely to get—exactly the opposite of what happens in the private sector, in which those who successfully meet the needs of their fellow men are rewarded with profits, and those who poorly anticipate consumer demand are punished with losses.

Take arts funding, for example. Some Americans appear to believe that there would be no arts in America were it not for the National Endowment for the Arts (NEA), an institution created in 1965. They cannot imagine things being done any other way, even though they *were* done another way throughout our country's existence, and throughout most of mankind's history. While the government requested $121 million for the NEA in 2006, private donations to the arts totaled $2.5 *billion* that year, dwarfing the NEA budget. The NEA represents a tiny fraction of all arts funding, a fact few Americans realize. Freedom works after all. And that money is almost certainly better spent than government money: NEA funds go not necessarily to the best artists, but to people who happen to be good at filling out government grant applications. I have my doubts that the same people populate both categories.

Alexis de Tocqueville was very impressed, when he visited our country in the nineteenth century, to see how many voluntary associations Americans had formed in order to achieve common goals. "The political associations which exist in the United States are only a single feature in the midst of the immense assemblage of associations in that country," he wrote. "Wherever, at the head of some new undertaking, you see the Government in France, or a man of rank in England, in the United States you will be sure to find an association." De Tocqueville admired "the extreme skill with which the inhabitants of the United States succeed in proposing a common object to the exertions of a great many men, and in getting them voluntarily to pursue it."

That may be all well and good for the arts and the like, some may say, but private efforts could never substitute for gigantic government budgets for various forms of welfare. But private assistance would not *need* to match these budgets dollar for dollar. As much as 70 percent of welfare budgets has been eaten up by bureaucracy. Moreover, government programs are far more easily abused, and the money they dispense more readily becomes a destructive habit, than with more local or private forms of assistance.

Why would we expect a system based on legal plunder, as ours is, to be a net benefit to the poor or middle class, in whose name so many government schemes are enacted? Every one of the special benefits, on behalf of which hundreds of millions of dollars are expended on lobbyists every year, makes goods more expensive, companies less efficient and competitive, and the economy more sluggish. Given that the politically influential and well connected—neither of which includes the middle class or the poor—are the ones who tend to win privileges and loot from government, I do not understand why we take for granted that the net result of all this looting is good for those who are lower on the economic ladder. And when the loot is paid for by printing money and causing inflation, which (as I show in the chapter on money) disproportionately harms the most vulnerable, the suggestion that the least prosperous are helped by all this intervention collapses into outright farce.

To get an appreciation for the difference between public and private administration in terms of bureaucracy and cost-effectiveness, consider this. The Brookings Institution's John Chubb once investigated the number of bureaucrats working in the central administration offices of the New York City public schools. Six telephone calls finally yielded someone who knew the answer, but that person was not allowed to disclose it. Another six calls later, Chubb had at last pinned down someone who knew the answer *and* could tell him what it was: there were 6,000 bureaucrats working in the central office.

Then Chubb called the Archdiocese of New York, to find out the figure there. (The city's Catholic schools educated one-fifth as many students as did the government-run schools.) Chubb's first telephone call was taken by someone who did not know the answer. Here we go again, he thought. But after a moment she said, "Wait a minute; let me count." Her answer: 26.

Now, whatever its moral and philosophical attractiveness, the free economy I have just proposed, in which no one is allowed to use government power to loot anyone else, is sometimes criticized as a "pro-business" philosophy that favors the well-to-do. This criticism could not be more off target. As I have said, businessmen, too, want special favors from government and lobby energetically for all kinds of wealth transfers to themselves. Very rarely does a business owner come to my congressional office to congratulate me on my fidelity to the Constitution. They come by because they want something, and what they want is usually not authorized by the Constitution.

I do not claim that businessmen as a class are underhanded or wicked, since I do not believe in making prejudicial generalizations about any group. I am saying only that they are just as likely as anyone else to favor government intervention on their behalf. I have nothing but respect and admiration for honest businessmen. Their contributions to our society are indispensable and almost completely unsung. The entrepreneur who risks everything he has in order to realize a dream—and improve our lives in the process—is engaged in a worthy and honorable pursuit that earns him precious little respect in our society. Economic historian Burton Folsom makes a useful distinction between market entrepreneurs, who grow wealthy when the public freely purchases what they have to sell, and political entrepreneurs, who grow wealthy because government cripples their competitors or grants them a monopoly. Folsom even shows that some of our most effective and admirable businessmen have succeeded in the face of rivals who enjoyed government subsidies and privileges.

I cannot finish a discussion of looting without mentioning the income tax. In another chapter I explain my opposition to the military draft, an institution based on the idea that the government owns its citizens and may direct their destinies against their will. The income tax implies the same thing: government owns you, and graciously allows you to keep whatever percentage of the fruits of your labor it chooses. Such an idea is incompatible with the principles of a free society.

Robert Nozick, the renowned twentieth-century political philosopher, minced no words when it came to the taxation of earnings from labor. How, he demanded to know, was this any different from forced labor? In America, the average citizen in effect does unremunerated work for the various levels of government for the equivalent of six months out of the year. People who favor this system should be honest about what they are saying: we have the right to force you to work against your will. Strip away the civics-class platitudes about "contributions" to "society," which are mere obfuscations designed to engineer the people's consent to the system, and that is what the income tax amounts to.

Frank Chodorov, a great stalwart of the old Right, put it this way:

> The citizen is sovereign only when he can retain and enjoy
> the fruits of his labor. If the government has first claim on

his property he must learn to genuflect before it. When the right of property is abrogated, all the other rights of the individual are undermined, and to speak of the sovereign citizen who has no absolute right of property is to talk nonsense. It is like saying that the slave is free because he is allowed to do anything he wants to do (even vote, if you wish) except to own what he produces.

With a consensus not yet established behind the abolition of the income tax (although I have never ceased voting and speaking on behalf of such an outcome), I have done my best to eliminate income and other taxation in as many specific cases as possible, in order at least to make dents in the edifice in the meantime. For instance, I have proposed, for all those whose income consists largely of tips, that income in the form of tips be exempt from income taxation. I have proposed that America's teachers be granted tax credits, thereby increasing their salaries. I have proposed that people with terminal illnesses be exempt from Social Security taxes while they struggle for their lives. (There is surely no moral justification for taxing people who are trying to maintain their very lives.)

What we should work toward, however, is abolishing the income tax and replacing it not with a national sales tax, but with nothing. Right now the federal government is funded by excise taxes, corporate income taxes, payroll taxes, the individual income tax, and miscellaneous other sources. Abolishing the income tax on individuals would cut government revenue by about 40 percent. I have heard the breathless claims about how radical that is—and compared to the trivial changes we are accustomed to seeing in government, I suppose it is. But in absolute terms, is it really so radical? In order to imagine what it would be like to live in a country with a federal budget 40 percent lower than the federal budget of 2007, it would be necessary to go all the way back to . . . 1997.

Would it really be so hard to imagine living in 1997 again? In return, we would have an economy so robust and dynamic that it would doubtless shatter even my own optimistic expectations. And we would once and for all have repudiated the totalitarian assumptions at the heart of the income tax.

How, by the way, did we ever let ourselves be talked into such a thing? The income tax was first proposed for several reasons. The tariff, from which the federal government received most of its funding, was for a variety of reasons bringing in a decreased revenue. At the same time, federal expenditures were going up, thanks in part to an increase in the military budget.

An alternative had to be found. At the time, many Americans viewed the tariff as an unfair tax that burdened them as consumers and benefited big business by sheltering it from foreign competition. A tax on incomes, the argument went, would at last force the rich to pay their share. And that's just how the income tax was pitched to the people: tax relief for you, in the form of lower tariffs, and a tax increase for the rich. Do not worry, people were told. Only the richest of the rich will ever pay the income tax.

That phony promise didn't last long. Within a few years, tax rates had shot through the roof, and classes of people who had thought they would never be taxed found themselves paying as well. And by the 1920s the tariff was raised again anyway, so the people wound up getting the worst of both worlds.

Now, plenty of politicians talk a good game about low taxes, and some even claim to want to decrease spending as well. Few seem to mean it, if their voting records are any indication. But if we want more economic freedom and a healthy and robust economy, serious inroads need to be made into federal spending. Otherwise, tax cuts will simply lead to more borrowing, more inflation, and the continued decline of the dollar. As I write, we are paying about $1.4 billion every day just for the interest on the national debt. Because our government refuses to live within its means, every single day we spend $1.4 billion and receive absolutely nothing in return.

But instead of talking seriously about how we might restore fiscal sanity to the federal budget, the political establishment tries to distract us with phony issues like the debate over "earmarks," legislative provisions that direct federal money to local projects. One need not look very hard to find examples of abuses of earmarks. But even if all earmarks were eliminated we would not necessarily save a single penny in the federal budget. Earmarks are funded from spending levels that have been determined before a single earmark is agreed to, so spending levels remain the same with or without earmarks.

By eliminating earmarks designated by members of Congress, all we would accomplish would be to transfer the funding decision process to federal bureaucrats and away from elected representatives. In a flawed system, earmarks can at least allow residents of congressional districts to have a greater role in allocating federal funds—their tax dollars—than if the money is apportioned behind locked doors by bureaucrats.

The real problem, and one that was unfortunately not addressed in 2007's earmark dispute, is the size of the federal government and the amount of money we are spending in these appropriations bills. Cutting even a million dollars from an appropriations bill that spends hundreds of billions will make no appreciable difference in the size of government, which is doubtless why politicians and the media are so eager to have us waste our time on this.

There is a danger that supporters of limited government will focus on this trivial question and neglect the much more important and difficult battle of returning the federal government to spending levels more in line with its constitutional functions. Without taking a serious look at the actual total spending in these appropriations bills, we will miss the real threat to our economic security.

The kind of spending cuts we obviously need will not be easy, since our government has encouraged so many Americans to become dependent on federal programs. These programs cannot survive much longer without a financial collapse. Our national debt, now nine trillion dollars, does not include the unfunded liabilities to programs like Social Security and Medicare that will come due in the coming decades to the tune of another $50 trillion. It is simply impossible to fulfill those promises. The level of taxation necessary to fund a figure like that would destroy the American economy and dramatically shrink the productive base from which those funds could be drawn.

David Walker, the comptroller general at the U.S. Government Accountability Office, tells us that Social Security and Medicare are headed for disaster because of demographic trends and rising health care costs. The number of younger taxpayers for each older retiree will continue to decline. The demand for "free" prescription drugs under Medicare will explode. If present trends continue, by 2040 the entire federal budget will be consumed by Social Security and Medicare. *Forty percent of our en-*

tire private-sector output will need to go to just these two programs. The only options for balancing the budget would be cutting total federal spending by about 60 percent, or doubling federal taxes.

Furthermore, Walker asserts, we cannot grow our way out of this problem. Faster economic growth can only delay the inevitable hard choices. To close the long-term entitlement gap, the U.S. economy would have to grow by double digits every year for the next 75 years.

Issues like these are predictably portrayed as contests between generous souls who want to provide for their fellow men on the one hand, and misers and misanthropes who care nothing for the suffering of their fellow citizens on the other. I should not have to point out that this is an absurd caricature. The fact is, *we do not have the resources to sustain these programs in the long run.* There is no way around this simple fact, a fact politicians consistently ignore or conceal in order to tell Americans what they think their fellow countrymen want to hear.

In the short run, in order to provide for those we have taught to be dependent, such programs could survive. My own suggestion is to fund this transition period by scaling back our unsustainable overseas commitments, saving hundreds of billions from the nearly one trillion dollars our empire is costing us every year, and in the process streamlining our overstretched military and making it more efficient and effective. That is the only place where we can easily save money, applying some of the savings to these domestic programs and the rest to debt reduction.

Our out-of-control welfare state also helps account for the scope of our illegal immigration problem. When you subsidize something, you get more of it, and by offering free medical care and other services, as well as the prospect of amnesty, we get more illegal immigration. Meanwhile, hospitals have begun closing as our states and localities struggle to pay the bills. That is one reason that the libertarian economist Milton Friedman once said, "You cannot simultaneously have free immigration and a welfare state." John Hospers, the Libertarian Party's first presidential candidate and the author of its Statement of Principles, has taken the same position.

And once again, the state divides rather than unifies. There would be far less hostility toward immigrants if the perception did not exist that they were getting something for nothing, while the rest of America struggles to make ends meet. There would likewise be less hostility if we had a more robust economy—which we absolutely would if we followed the advice in this book. When, thanks to government policy, the economy is shaky, as it is now with the housing bubble bursting and inflation on the rise, it is all the easier to hold up immigrants as the scapegoats for people's economic woes, thereby letting the incompetents and shysters who make our economic policy off the hook.

Excessive government spending has done more than just put us in debt. Charles Murray offers us a useful thought experiment that illustrates the welfare state's enervating effects on our communities and our character. Imagine that the programs that constituted the federal "safety net" were all of a sudden abolished, and for whatever reason could not be revived. And pretend also that the states chose not to replace them with programs of their own, which they almost certainly would. The questions Murray wants us to focus on are these: How would you respond? Would you be more or less likely to volunteer at a food bank? Would you be more or less likely to volunteer at a literacy center? If you were a lawyer or physician, would you be more or less likely to offer pro bono services?

We would all answer yes to these questions, wouldn't we? But then we need to ask ourselves: why aren't we doing these things already? And the answer is that we have bought into the soul-killing logic of the welfare state: somebody else is doing it for me. I don't need to give of myself, since a few scribbles on a tax form fulfill my responsibility toward my fellow man. Do our responsibilities as human beings really extend no farther than this?

In the days before Medicare and Medicaid, for instance, the poor and elderly were admitted to hospitals at about the same rate they are now, and received good care. As a physician I never accepted Medicare or Medicaid money from the government, and instead offered cut-rate or free services to those who could not afford care. Before those programs came into existence, every physician understood that he or she had a responsibility toward the less fortunate, and free medical care for the poor was the norm. Hardly anyone is aware of this today, since it doesn't fit into the typical, by-the-script story of government rescuing us from a predatory private sector. Laws and regulations that inflated the cost of medical services and imposed unreasonable liability standards on medical professionals even when they were acting in a volunteer capacity later made offering free care cost prohibitive, but free care for the poor was common at a time when America wasn't so "governmentish" (to borrow a word from William Penn). We have lost our belief that freedom works, because we no longer have the imagination to conceive of how a free people might solve its problems without introducing threats of violence—which is what government solutions ultimately amount to.

In *From Mutual Aid to Welfare State: Fraternal Societies and Social Services, 1890–1967*, historian David Beito uncovered some of the story of how people once cared for their needs in the absence of massive bureaucracies and the financial chaos and moral hazard they inevitably cause. Beito focuses particular attention on fraternal organizations, which in decades past provided all kinds of services for their members that we now assume must be handled by government. With strength in numbers, such organizations were able to negotiate with doctors and get very inexpensive health care as well.

On the other hand, just about everyone is unhappy with the health care system we have now, a system some people wrongly blame on the free market. To the contrary, our system is shot through with government intervention, regulation, mandates, and other distortions that have put us in this unenviable situation.

It is easy to forget that for decades the United States had a health care system that was the envy of the world. We had the finest doctors and hospitals, patients received high-quality, affordable medical care, and thousands of privately funded charities provided health services for the poor. I worked in an emergency room where nobody was turned away for lack of funds. People had insurance policies for serious health problems but paid cash for routine doctor visits. That makes sense: insurance is intended to protect against unforeseen and catastrophic events like fire, floods, or grave illness. Insurance, in short, is supposed to measure risk. It has nothing to do with that now. Something has obviously gone wrong with the system when we need insurance for routine visits and checkups, which are entirely predictable parts of our lives.

Today most Americans obtain health care either through a Health Maintenance Organization (HMO) or similar managed-care organization, or through Medicare or Medicaid. Since it is very hard to make actuarial estimates for routine health care, HMOs charge most members a similar monthly premium. Because HMOs always want to minimize their costs, they often deny payment for various drugs, treatments, and procedures. Similarly, Medicare does not have unlimited funds, so it generally covers only a portion of any costs. The result of all this is that doctors and patients cannot simply decide what treatment is appropriate. Instead, they constantly find themselves being second-guessed by HMO accountants and government bureaucrats.

When a third party is paying the bills and malpractice lawsuits loom, doctors have every incentive to maximize costs and order all possible tests and treatments. The incentive to cut costs is lost, as physicians (now working essentially as low-level employees) seek to make as much as they can in the new corporate environment and charge the maximum the HMOs allow. Before 1965, physicians and hospitals (like all other private entities competing for your dollar) strove to charge the minimum; because payment now comes so largely from third parties, they instead charge the maximum. At the same time, patients suffer when legitimate and necessary treatment is denied. HMOs have become corporate, bureaucratic middlemen in our health care system, driving up costs while degrading the quality of medical care. In all other industries, technology has nearly always led to lower prices—except in health care, thanks to the managed-care system that has been forced upon us.

In fact, with costs skyrocketing due to this system, more and more Americans are actually traveling overseas to get high-quality, inexpensive health care—half a million of them took this route in 2005 alone. It is not unusual to be able to get an operation in

India, at the hands of Western-trained physicians, for 60 percent less than it would cost in the United States.

The story behind the creation of the HMOs is a classic illustration of what economist Ludwig von Mises once said: government interventions create unintended consequences that lead to calls for further intervention, and so on into a destructive spiral of more and more government control. During the early 1970s, Congress embraced HMOs in order to address concerns about rising health care costs. But it was Congress itself that had caused health care costs to spiral by removing control over the health care dollar from so many consumers in the 1960s, and thus eliminating any incentive to pay attention to costs when selecting health care. Now, Congress wants to intervene yet again to address problems caused by HMOs, the product of still earlier interventions.

Now that HMOs are all but universally unpopular, the very politicians who brought them to us are joining the bandwagon to denounce them, hoping the American people will forget, or never be told, that the federal government itself virtually mandated HMOs in the first place. The tax code excludes health insurance from taxation when purchased by an employer, but not when purchased by an individual. In addition, the HMO Act of 1973 forced all but the smallest employers to offer HMOs to their employees. The combined result was the illogical coupling of employment and health insurance, which often leaves the unemployed without needed catastrophic coverage. As usual, then, government intervention into the market caused unintended, undesired consequences, but politicians blame the HMOs instead of the interventions that helped create them. Consumer complaints about insurers and HMOs compel politicians to draft new laws and more regulations to curry voter favor. More regulations breed more costs, limiting more choices, causing more anguish—and the cycle continues.

The most obvious way to break this cycle is to get the government out of the business of meddling in health care, which was far more affordable and accessible before government got involved. Short of that, and more politically feasible in the immediate run, is to allow consumers and their doctors to pull themselves out of the system through medical savings accounts. Under this system, consumers could save pretax dollars in special accounts. Those dollars would be used to pay for health care expenses, with patients negotiating directly with the physicians of their choice for the care they choose, without regard for HMO rules or a bureaucrat's decision. The incentive for the physician is that he gets paid as the service is rendered, rather than having to wait months for an HMO or insurance provider's billing cycle.

With the cash for the MSAs coming from pretax dollars, most Americans could afford deposits that would cover routine expenses that families experience in a year. Insurance would tend to return to its normal function of providing for large-scale, unanticipated occurrences, and would become far more affordable.

Even now, though, it is possible for physicians to operate outside this crazy system if they make a special effort to do so. Several years ago I had a chance to meet Dr. Robert Berry, who had come to Washington to offer testimony before the congressional Joint Economic Committee, of which I am a member. Dr. Berry had opened a low-cost health clinic in rural Tennessee. The clinic does not accept insurance, Medicare, or Medicaid, a policy that allows Dr. Berry to treat patients without interference from third-party government bureaucrats or HMO administrators. He and his patients can therefore decide for themselves on appropriate treatments.

In other words, Dr. Berry practices medicine as most doctors did 40 years ago, when patients paid cash for ordinary services and had inexpensive catastrophic insurance for serious injuries or illnesses.

Doing so affords him additional advantages as well. Freed from the bureaucracies of HMOs or government, he can focus on medicine rather than billing. By operating on a cash basis he lowers his overhead considerably, thereby making it possible to charge much lower prices than other doctors. He often charges just $35 dollars for routine maladies—only slightly more than the insurance co-pay that other offices charge. His affordable prices enable low-income patients to see him before minor problems become serious, and unlike most doctors, Dr. Berry sees patients the same day on a walk-in basis.

His patients are largely low-income working people who cannot afford health insurance but don't necessarily qualify for state assistance. Some of his uninsured patients have been forced to visit hospital emergency rooms for nonemergency treatment because no doctor would see them. Others disliked the long waits and inferior treatment they endured at government clinics.

And speaking of poor treatment, those who favor national health care schemes should take a good, hard look at our veterans' hospitals. There is your national health care. These institutions are a national disgrace. If this is the care the government dispenses to those it honors as its most heroic and admirable citizens, why should anyone else expect to be treated any better?

———

Americans have been given the impression that "regulation" is always a good thing, and that anyone who speaks of lessening the regulatory burden is an antisocial ogre who would sacrifice safety and human well-being for the sake of economic efficiency. If so much as one of the tens of thousands of pages in the Federal Register, which lists all federal regulations, were to be eliminated, we would all die instantly.

The real history of regulation is not so straightforward. Businesses have often called for regulation themselves, hopeful that their smaller competitors will have a more difficult time meeting regulatory demands. Special interests have helped to impose utterly senseless regulations that impose crushing burdens on private enterprise—far out of proportion to any benefit they are alleged to bring—but since those interests bear none of these burdens themselves, it costs them nothing to advocate them.

When Senator George McGovern retired from public life, he became the proprietor of a small Connecticut hotel called the Stratford Inn. Two and a half years later, the inn was forced to close. After his experience running his own business, former Senator McGovern had the honesty to wonder about the merits of all the regulations that, truth be told, he himself had helped to implement. "Legislators and government regulators must more carefully consider the economic and management burdens we have been imposing on U.S. business," he said. He continued:

As an innkeeper, I wanted excellent safeguards against a fire. But I was startled to be told that our two-story structure, which had large sliding doors opening from every guest room to all-concrete decks, required us to meet fire regulations more appropriate to the Waldorf-Astoria. A costly automatic sprinkler system and new exit doors were items that helped sink the Stratford Inn—items I was convinced added little to the safety of our guests and employees. And a critical promotional campaign never got off the ground, partly because my manager was forced to concentrate for days at a time on needlessly complicated tax forms for both the IRS and the state of Connecticut.

"I'm for protecting the health and well-being of both workers and consumers," McGovern went on. "I'm for a clean environment and economic justice. But I'm convinced we can pursue those worthy goals and still cut down vastly on the incredible paperwork, the complicated tax forms, the number of minute regulations, and the seemingly endless reporting requirements that afflict American business. Many businesses, especially small independents such as the Stratford Inn, simply can't pass such costs on to their customers and remain competitive or profitable."

He concluded: "If I were back in the U.S. Senate or in the White House, I would ask a lot of questions before I voted for any more burdens on the thousands of struggling businesses across the nation." That is an important lesson: government intervention into the economy cannot be assumed to be good and welcome and just.

But that is how it is portrayed in too many of our American

history classrooms. It is not unusual for American students to find their textbooks telling them that injustice was everywhere before the federal government, motivated by nothing but a deep commitment to the public good, intervened to save them from the wickedness of the free market. Alleged "monopolies" dictated prices to hapless consumers. Laborers were forced to accept ever-lower wages. And thanks to their superior economic position, giant corporations effortlessly parried the attempts of anyone foolish enough to try to compete with them.

Every single aspect of this story is false, though of course this version of our history continues to be peddled and believed. I don't blame people for believing it—it's the only rendition of events they're ever told, unless by some fluke they have learned where to look for the truth. But there is an agenda behind this silly comic-book version of history: to make people terrified of the "unfettered" free market, and to condition them to accept the ever-growing burdens that the political class imposes on the private sector as an unchangeable aspect of life that exists for their own good.

An argument we hear even now is that a hundred years ago, when the federal government was far smaller than it is today, people were much poorer and worked in less desirable conditions, while today, with a much larger federal government and far more regulation in place, people are much more prosperous. This is a classic case of the *post hoc, ergo propter hoc* fallacy. This fallacy is committed whenever we carelessly assume that because outcome B occurred *after* action A, then B was *caused* by A. If people are more prosperous today, that must be because government saved them from the ravages of the free market.

But that is nonsense. *Of course* people were less prosperous a hundred years ago, but not for the reason fashionable opinion assumes. Compared to today, the American economy was starved for capital. The economy's productive capacity was minuscule by today's standards, and therefore very few goods per capita could be produced. The vast bulk of the population had to make do with much less than we take for granted today *because so little could be produced.* All the laws and regulations in the world cannot overcome constraints imposed by reality itself. No matter how much we tax the rich to redistribute wealth, in a capital-starved economy there is an extremely limited amount of wealth to redistribute.

The only way to increase everyone's standard of living is by increasing the amount of capital per worker. Additional capital makes workers more productive, which means they can produce more goods than before. When our economy becomes physically capable of producing vastly more goods, their abundance makes them more affordable in terms of dollars (if the Federal Reserve isn't inflating the money supply). Soaking the rich works for only so long: the rich eventually wise up and decide to hide their income, move away, or stop working so much. But investing in capital makes everyone better off. It is the only way we can all become wealthier. We are wealthier today because our economy is physically capable of producing so much more at far lower costs. And that's why, just from a practical point of view, it is foolish to levy taxes along any step of this process, because doing so sabotages the only way wealth can be created for everyone.

Prosperity comes not just from economic freedom at home, but also from the freedom to trade abroad. If free trade were not beneficial, it would make sense for us to "protect jobs" by buying only those goods produced entirely in our own towns. Or we could purchase only those goods produced on the streets where we live. Better still, we could restrict our purchases to things produced in our own households, buying all our products only from our own immediate family members. When the logic of trade restriction is taken to its natural conclusion, its impoverishing effects become too obvious to miss.

Frédéric Bastiat once wrote a satirical petition to the French parliament on behalf of candlemakers and related industries. He was seeking relief from "ruinous competition of a foreign rival who works under conditions so far superior to our own for the production of light that he is flooding the domestic market with it at an incredibly low price." The "foreign rival" he was speaking of was the sun, which was unfairly giving away light for free. The relief sought was a law requiring the closing of all blinds to shut out the sunlight and thereby stimulate the domestic candle industry. That is what so many fallacious arguments against free trade amount to.

In spite of my strong support for free trade, I have felt compelled to oppose many of the trade agreements that have appeared in recent years. For instance, although I was not in Congress at the time, I opposed both the North American Free Trade Agreement and the World Trade Organization, both of which were heavily favored by the political establishment. Initial grounds for suspicion was the sheer length of the text of these agreements: no free-trade agreement needs to be 20,000 pages long.

Many, though not all, supporters of the free market supported these agreements. Very different was the situation nearly six decades ago when the International Trade Organization was up for debate. At that time, conservatives and libertarians agreed that supranational trade bureaucracies with the power to infringe upon

American sovereignty were undesirable and unnecessary. Business-man Philip Cortney, a close friend of the great free-market econo-mist Ludwig von Mises, led the charge against the WTO with his book *The Economic Munich*. Henry Hazlitt, author of the libertar-ian classic *Economics in One Lesson*, included Cortney's book against the WTO in The Free Man's Library, his annotated read-ing list of books important to the study of freedom.

In 1994, Newt Gingrich, who supported the WTO, spoke with rare candor about the amount of authority the United States was transferring to a supranational organization:

> I am just saying that we need to be honest about the fact that we are transferring from the United States at a practical level significant authority to a new organization. This is a transformational moment. I would feel better if the people who favor this would just be honest about the scale of change. . . . This is not just another trade agreement. This is adopting something which twice, once in the 1940s and once in the 1950s, the U.S. Congress rejected. I am not even saying that we should reject it; I, in fact, lean toward it. But I think we have to be very careful, because it is a very big transfer of power.

To establish genuine free trade, no such transfer of power is necessary. True free trade does not require treaties or agreements between governments. On the contrary, true free trade occurs in the *absence* of government intervention in the free flow of goods across borders. Organizations like the WTO and NAFTA repre-sent government-managed trade schemes, not free trade. The WTO, purported to exist to lower tariffs, is actually the agency that grants permission for tariffs to be applied when complaints of dumping are levied. Government-managed trade is inherently political, meaning that politicians and bureaucrats determine who wins and loses in the marketplace.

Granting quasi-governmental international bodies the power to make decisions about American trade rules compromises American sovereignty in dangerous and unacceptable ways. Congress has changed American tax laws for the sole reason that the World Trade Organization decided that our rules unfairly impacted the European Union. I recall a congressional session in which, with hundreds of tax bills languishing in the House Ways and Means Committee, the one bill drafted strictly to satisfy the WTO was brought to the floor and passed with great urgency.

In one case, the WTO sided with the Europeans against American tax law, which offered tax breaks to American companies doing business overseas. According to the European Union, the Foreign Sales Corporation program, established under President Reagan in 1984, is now an "illegal subsidy," a view that a WTO appellate panel shared. The WTO's Orwellian ruling declared that allowing a company to keep more of its own money through lower taxes was a "subsidy." As a matter of fact, the program was moreover really just compensating (and only partially at that) for unfair U.S. taxes on corporations for profits earned overseas, a disability that our foreign competitors do not have to confront from their own governments.

What this meant, in plain English, was that high-tax Europe, upset at lower-tax America, decided that the way to level the playing field was to force America to raise her taxes. Pascal Lamy, the trade czar of the European Union, actually visited with influential members of Congress in order to determine whether a new tax bill was being crafted to his satisfaction. If Mr. Lamy, a member of the French Socialist Party, had been unsatisfied with the changes made to our tax code, he threatened to unleash a European trade war against U.S. imports. In effect he was a foreign bureaucrat acting as a shadow legislator by intervening in our lawmaking process. And to no one's surprise, Congress raced to comply with the WTO ruling that American tax rules must be changed in order to bring them into harmony with "international law."

This outrageous affront to our national sovereignty was of course predictable when we joined the WTO. During congressional debates we were assured that entry into the organization posed no threat to our sovereignty. A well-known libertarian think tank, where you might expect some skepticism of a supranational bureaucracy managing trade, offered us this rosy description: "The WTO's dispute settlement mechanism helps nations resolve trade disputes without resorting to costly trade wars. The system relies on voluntary compliance and does not compromise national sovereignty." That was nonsense. A Congressional Research Service report was quite clear about the consequences of our membership: "As a member of the WTO, the United States does commit to act in accordance with the rules of the multi-lateral body. It is legally obligated to insure that national laws do not conflict with WTO rules."

The WTO has given us the worst of both worlds: we've sacrificed national sovereignty by changing our domestic laws at the behest of an international body, yet we still face trade wars over a variety of products. If anything, the WTO makes trade relations worse by providing our foreign competitors with a collective means to attack U.S. trade interests.

And let us not forget that the Constitution grants Congress, and Congress alone, the authority to regulate trade and craft tax laws. Congress cannot cede that authority to the WTO or any other international body. Nor can the president legally sign any treaty that purports to do so. Our Founders never intended for America to become entangled in global trade schemes, and they certainly never intended to have our domestic laws overridden by international bureaucrats.

Now, while free trade should be embraced, foreign aid should be absolutely rejected. Constitutional, moral, and practical arguments compel such a view. Constitutional authorization for such programs is at best dubious. Morally, I cannot justify the violent seizure of property from Americans in order to redistribute that property to a foreign government—and usually one that is responsible for the appalling material condition of its people. Surely we can agree that Americans ought not to be doing forced labor on behalf of other regimes, and that is exactly what foreign aid is.

For those who find arguments like these abstract and remote, there is a more practical argument against foreign aid. International welfare has not worked any better than domestic welfare, despite the trillions spent in each case. Foreign aid, however pure the intentions that may have motivated it, has been a reactionary device by which truly loathsome leaders have been strengthened and kept in power. Trillions of dollars later, the results of development aid programs are so bad that even the *New York Times*, which admits nothing, has acknowledged that the programs haven't worked. No wonder Kenyan economist James Shikwati, when asked about development aid programs to Africa, has been telling the West, "For God's sake, please just stop."

The greatest prophet of the foreign aid debacle, who was ignored until his predictions came true—as inevitably as night follows day—in the 1980s and beyond, was the late Peter Bauer of the London School of Economics. It is to his extraordinary corpus of work that I refer anyone who actually cares about helping people in need, as opposed to repeating mindless slogans or reflexively giving government programs the benefit of the doubt.

On the other hand, the economic success stories of the past half century have arisen not from foreign aid but out of the extraordinary workings of the free market, the great engine of human well-being that everyone is taught to hate. I would choose freedom even if it meant less prosperity, but thankfully we do not face such a choice. Look at the countries that have risen from poverty to affluence and you will find places where economic freedom has a fighting chance, and contracts and property are respected. Look at Botswana, which has one of the freest economies—and among the most prosperous people—on the African continent. In South America look at Chile, whose people enjoy a standard of living of which most peoples elsewhere on the continent can only dream. Look at the economic miracle in Ireland, or the fantastic growth rates in Estonia. Let's quit pretending that we don't know how to make people prosperous, when the evidence is all around us.

The ideas of liberty and a free economy have not spread with equal force everywhere in the world; nor have they been implemented with consistency. The results have been overwhelming all the same. Between 1980 and 2000, India's real GDP per head more than doubled, and in China real income per capita rose by 400 percent. Poverty in China went from 28 percent in 1978 to 9 percent in 1998. In India, it fell from 51 percent in 1977–1978 to 26 percent in 1999–2000. "Never before," writes economist

Martin Wolf, "have so many people—or so large a proportion of the world's population—enjoyed such large rises in their standards of living."

Poverty has also been reduced throughout the world as a whole. In 1820, over 80 percent of the world's population lived in what the literature calls "extreme poverty." By 1950 that figure was 50 percent. By 1992 it was down to 24 percent. (In the United States, poverty declined consistently from 1950 until 1968, when supposedly antipoverty programs first began to receive significant funding. Since then, the poverty figures have stagnated in spite of trillions of dollars spent.)

Never before in the history of the world have so many people seen such an improvement in their living standards. And these wonderful results have come about quite in spite of official development aid programs devised in the West. They are, instead, the natural result of the market economy. Forget about all the propaganda, the sloganeering, the misinformation, the willful misunderstanding of how the market works, all of which characterize fashionable opinion on the subject. These are facts—and they should not be unexpected facts, if we understand sound economics.

If Americans knew the real story of foreign aid and how it has deformed recipient economies, aided repressive regimes, and even contributed to violent strife, they would oppose it even more strongly than they already do. If they knew about the record of the International Monetary Fund and the World Bank when it comes to helping developing countries, they would be similarly appalled. At long last, these seemingly untouchable programs need to be called into question, and then, in the name of liberty and humanity, discarded forever.

Mine is an "isolationist" position only to those who believe that the world's peoples can interact with each other only through their governments, or only through the intermediary of a supranational bureaucracy. That unspoken assumption is dangerous and dehumanizing. There is nothing isolationist about opposing coercive government-to-government wealth transfers. Individuals who wish to contribute directly to some worthy cause abroad—and Third World governments whose destructive policies have kept their peoples in miserable poverty are not such a cause—should be perfectly at liberty to do so. In fact, a recent Hudson Institute study found that in 2006, American citizens voluntarily contributed three times more to help people overseas than did the United States government. Freedom works.

The issues I have raised so far show how important it is for a free people to possess a sound understanding of economics. I myself identify with a school of economic thought known as the Austrian School of economics, whose key twentieth-century figures included Ludwig von Mises, F. A. Hayek, Murray Rothbard, and Hans Sennholz. The Austrian School has enjoyed something of a renaissance ever since Hayek, one of its brightest lights, won the Nobel Prize in 1974. And with all kinds of financial bubbles bursting, from the dot-coms a decade ago to housing today, financial analysts have been particularly interested in the Austrian message, especially since the Austrians were among the only ones who consistently warned about those bubbles. Mises himself was practically alone in 1928 when he insisted that not only had permanent prosperity *not* arrived (as the mainstream of the economics profession had been foolishly assuring everyone throughout the decade), but that a great economic downturn was inevitable.

I have always had a deep personal admiration for Ludwig von

Mises, one of the great economists of all time. His book *Human Action: A Treatise on Economics*, while challenging, will bring great intellectual pleasure to anyone who thirsts for truth. (Beginners should consider starting with some of his simpler works intended for general audiences.) And it was not just Mises' brilliance that moved me but also his moral courage. Mises adopted Virgil's motto as his own: "Do not give in to evil, but proceed ever more boldly against it." Mises never sought advancement by telling the political class what it wanted to hear. Economics, said Mises, is "a challenge to the conceit of those in power. An economist can never be a favorite of autocrats and demagogues. With them he is always the mischief-maker, and the more they are inwardly convinced that his objections are well founded, the more they hate him." And the Nazis did hate him, both because he was Jewish and because of his denunciation, in the name of free-market economics, of the Nazi economic program.

Mises believed in free trade, toleration, and peace—exactly the opposite of the nationalistic, autarkic philosophy of the National Socialists, or Nazis, whose ugly creed grew more and more influential as the 1930s wore on. In 1934 Mises accepted a position as a professor of international economic relations at the University of Geneva's Graduate Institute of International Studies. Four years later, the Nazis destroyed his papers and library back in Vienna. By 1940, with Switzerland surrounded by countries under the control of the Axis powers, Mises fled to the United States. When he arrived he had no teaching position waiting for him and no resources, and he spoke no English. He was 60.

By that point he had produced some of his most enduring work: in addition to writing two major treatises, *The Theory of Money and Credit* and *Socialism*, he had published a vast array of influential articles and mentored countless young students who went on to be the finest economic thinkers of their day. And yet, against all odds, still more was to come after his sixtieth year, when his personal and professional situation seemed so dire. In the 1940s he released *Omnipotent Government*, his study of the Nazi phenomenon; *Bureaucracy*; and his magnum opus, *Human Action*, a 900-page work he wrote in English, a language of which he had not known one word in 1940. The 1950s saw the release of the fourth of his great treatises, *Theory and History*.

Mises continued to swim against the tide until his death in 1973, teaching and theorizing about freedom at a time when Keynesian and other kinds of central planners dominated academic economics. While most of those names are now forgotten, Mises and his legacy live on, as his work influences new generations of intellectuals who see through the lies of planners and other tyrants, and understand the value of liberty.

In 1982 I was honored to play a small role in founding the Ludwig von Mises Institute, the world's foremost center for the study and promotion of free market economics in the tradition of the Austrian School. Through its programs and publications the Institute has played a critical role in spreading the ideas of a free society, sound money, and peace. Its Web site, Mises.org, contains so many resources—lectures, courses, articles, and even whole books—that you could spend a lifetime learning from it.

I sometimes hear people say that they find economics boring. That almost always means they've never read the Austrians, whose work brims with intellectual excitement. (Again, see my reading list at the end of this book for suggestions.)

Some people falsely believe that advocates of the free market must be opponents of the environment. We care only about economic efficiency, the argument goes, and have no regard for the consequences of pollution and other examples of environmental degradation. But a true supporter of private property and personal responsibility cannot be indifferent to environmental damage, and should view it as a form of unjustified aggression that must be punished or enjoined, or dealt with in some other way that is mutually satisfactory to all parties. Private business should not have the right to socialize its costs by burdening other people with the by-products of its operations.

Economist Martin Anderson puts it this way. Dumping garbage on your neighbor's lawn is wrong. But pollution is really just another form of garbage. For that reason, proposals to charge pollution fees, which get higher the greater the pollution, neglect the demands of justice. Anderson compares it to taxing thieves as a way of giving them an economic incentive not to burglarize your home. If the practice is wrong, the law should treat it as such. "If a firm creates pollution without first entering into an agreement, or if the parties cannot come to an agreement fixing the cost and degree of pollution, then the court system could be used to assess damages," say economists Walter Block and Robert W. McGee.

In fact, that's how American law used to treat pollution. But a series of nineteenth-century nuisance cases changed that: the courts suddenly decided that a certain level of pollution could be allowed for the sake of the greater good. The implication was that if, for example, a few farmers had their property destroyed by passing trains, that was just the price of progress. (Easy for them to say!) These cases allowed private industry to invade the property rights of others and deprived those others of legal recourse. I do not see this as a free-market outcome.*

Imagine if the previous legal approach to pollution had not been overturned, and polluters continued to be legally liable for any such invasive practices. Block and McGee suggest that we would long ago have "begun enjoying a non-pollution-intensive technology where there were no open-ended smokestacks. Instead, these pipes would have led back to chemical cisterns, the latter to capture otherwise errant soot particles." This approach would also have encouraged the growth of an environmental forensics industry that would allow us to identify those responsible for pollution by determining its exact source, just as DNA evidence now permits us to identify rapists and murderers.

Campaign finance reform was the subject of fierce debate in America not long ago. Yet the debate missed the point. As long as we have a government that can exploit peaceful, hardworking Americans on behalf of special interests, as long as it can make or break any American business with (for example) tax policy, politically motivated antitrust prosecutions, and ill-considered regulation, and in general as long as economic winners and losers can be determined in Washington, people will want to assure their share of the loot by influencing the political process through

*I do not claim that pollution consisting of a few undetectable particles must be prohibited, or that no airplanes would have the right to travel high above people's homes. These are legitimate matters for the courts, where such matters have been properly decided in the past.

money. Campaign finance reform focuses on the symptom rather than the cause.

This is one reason I was so skeptical when friends urged me to run for president. There are far more interest groups lobbying in Washington for special benefits and privileges than most Americans can imagine. I do not oppose just this one or that one. I oppose the whole apparatus, the whole immoral system by which we use government to exploit our fellow citizens on behalf of our own interests. For someone like me to win, there would have to be enough Americans who believed in freedom to be able to offset the combined power of interest groups that have grown accustomed to treating the people as a resource to be drained for private gain. Were there really enough people for that task?

What moves me the most when I think about my supporters in my presidential campaign are the staggering efforts and creative energies—extraordinary and unprecedented, as far as I can see—that they expended on behalf of a message that promised them no special benefits, no loot taken from their fellow men. The message promises only freedom, and no special privileges for anyone. No one is surprised that people donate to a political campaign in the hopes of receiving some special favor if the candidate wins. I was quite surprised, on the other hand, at how many would donate, volunteer, and vote in pursuit of nothing other than freedom, and the prosperity it naturally brings.

CHAPTER 5

Civil Liberties and Personal Freedom

Freedom means not only that our economic activity ought to be free and voluntary, but that government should stay out of our personal affairs as well. In fact, freedom means that we understand liberty as an indivisible whole. Economic freedom and personal liberty are not divisible. How do you plan to exercise your right to free speech if you're not allowed the economic freedom to acquire the supplies necessary to disseminate your views? Likewise, how can we expect to enjoy privacy rights if our property rights are insecure?

Government should respect our right to privacy, rather than invading it on phony pretenses. It should observe traditional legal norms when dealing with criminal suspects. And instead of trying to correct our bad habits at the point of a gun, it should defer to families and the normal channels of civil society to instruct people in moral conduct.

The war on terror has awakened more Americans than ever to the way government exploits fear, and even its own failures, to justify eroding our civil liberties. Examples are all too plentiful.

For instance, only well after the fact did Americans discover that their government had been defying the law by carrying out warrantless surveillance of Americans' international telephone conversations. After sitting on the story for a year, the *New York Times* went public with the program in December 2005.

That in itself should give us pause: why, in a free society with a supposedly independent media, did arguably the most influential newspaper in the United States keep Americans in the dark about a program like this? The answer we were given involved unspecified national security concerns that the *Times* supposedly did not want to jeopardize. But that explanation does not hold water at all. We may safely assume that terrorists are clever enough to realize that our government is listening in on their conversations, even without the *Times* telling them so. The very name of the Foreign Intelligence Surveillance Act (FISA) of 1978 is a dead giveaway.

As far as we have been told, the only way that this program, administered by the U.S. National Security Agency (NSA), diverged from previous intelligence efforts is that this one operated without FISA warrants—warrants issued in secret by special courts, in conformity with the 1978 Act. Awareness of this aspect of the program would have done nothing to aid terrorists. FISA warrants are issued in secret anyway, so neither under FISA nor under the NSA program would a terrorist know for sure that the government was eavesdropping on his conversations.

It looks very much like the old story: the government says "national security" and the natural and normal skepticism that our Founding Fathers taught us to have toward the government is promptly abandoned. The simple and straightforward reason the executive branch wanted the program kept secret, its consistent obfuscation notwithstanding, seems to be that it violated the law.

The reasons we were given for why the program was necessary were at least as unconvincing as the *Times*'s defense of concealing it. On the one hand, we were told that the only targets of the program were people with links to terrorist organizations like al Qaeda. At the same time, we were told that the sheer number of targets made FISA warrant applications impracticable.

I believe that constitutional lawyer Glenn Greenwald has identified a fatal contradiction in these claims. If it is true that the executive branch knew the locations of so many people with al Qaeda links, why were they seeking merely to eavesdrop on their conversations? Why were they not arresting them instead? This, after all, is an administration that has detained people indefinitely, without charges, on the basis of sometimes shaky evidence of an al Qaeda connection. This time, we are supposed to believe that the administration had knowledge of countless al Qaeda figures and decided to let them remain free? Not plausible, and that is why it seems likely that the targets of this surveillance included many Americans who had no ties to al Qaeda or terrorism at all.

Then we were told that the program wasn't lawless after all—the president had been given this authority by Congress in the 2001 Authorization to Use Military Force (AUMF) that authorized military action in Afghanistan. It seems dubious that anyone in Congress at the time interpreted the AUMF as giving the president the power to engage in warrantless wiretapping in contravention of established law. According to Bruce Fein, deputy attorney general under President Reagan, that interpretation of AUMF would mean that it was also intended to authorize the president to "break and enter homes, open mail, torture detainees, or even open internment camps for American citizens in violation of federal statutes in order to gather foreign intelligence." It is not plausible to suggest that Congress would have intended to authorize such extreme measures by silence or remote implication. If this interpretation of AUMF were correct, moreover, parts of the Patriot Act would have been unnecessary. Finally, given that FISA, the existing law, deals explicitly and specifically with intelligence gathering, while AUMF says nothing at all about foreign intelligence, FISA would automatically trump AUMP as a matter of legal principle, even if the administration's interpretation were correct.

The administration itself didn't seem to take this argument seriously. When asked why, if the administration considered FISA inadequate to its purposes, it had not sought to amend it, Attorney General Alberto Gonzales frankly testified that they didn't think they would be able to win congressional approval for amendments to FISA. So they proceeded with the program anyway. That's problematic enough, but it also contradicts administration claims that AUMF gave them all the authority they needed. Why did they consider amending FISA in order to give themselves a power they supposedly already had?

Then, in yet another twist, we were told that NSA was carrying out what is known as "data mining," which amounts to combing through the communications of all Americans, and FISA could not accommodate this. Well, no, I should think not.

Finally, there is the argument that the president needs to be able to act with dispatch in order to pursue the targets he seeks. This argument also fails to persuade—existing law was extremely accommodating on this score, allowing for warrantless surveillance for days at a time in emergency situations.

What was the real reason for the program, then? Who was targeted and why? No answers to these questions have been forthcoming. Bland assurances that our leaders are trustworthy and good, and would never abuse powers they have secretly exercised in defiance of the law, can hardly be taken seriously by those who believe in a free society. Remember Jefferson's cautionary words about confidence in men: we should be on our guard against our government officials, binding them down from mischief by the chains of the Constitution. Government surveillance of individuals *has* been abused in the past, and it *has* targeted political opponents and the politically unpopular. That's why the safeguards that were flaunted here were established in the first place. Frank Church, who served as a U.S. senator from Idaho for a quarter of a century and who investigated and led the charge for reform of the surveillance powers of American intelligence agencies, was observing as early as 1975 that the NSA, if it fell into the wrong hands, could enable the government "to impose a total tyranny, and there would be no way to fight back."

This particular program was known as the Terrorist Surveillance Program, and it received a great deal of attention after its existence became public. What was frequently overlooked amid the ensuing controversy was that the executive branch apparently carried out even more invasive activities, but we never got any answers about those. When asked whether they had engaged in domestic wiretapping or carried out warrantless searches of people's homes or correspondence, officials have responded with carefully worded assurances that these things were not done *under the program then under discussion*—i.e., the Terrorist Surveillance Program. But were these things being done pursuant to some other program? No answer.

When then Attorney General Alberto Gonzales testified before the Senate Judiciary Committee in February 2006, for example, he dealt with questions about whether the administration had engaged in warrantless wiretapping of purely domestic calls. "Not under the program in which I'm testifying," came the reply. Such activity, the attorney general said, was "beyond the bound of the program which I'm testifying about today."

We do know that for some period of time between September 11, 2001, and March 2004, the executive branch was engaged in a kind of surveillance that was so at odds with American law that then Attorney General John Ashcroft, FBI Director Robert Mueller, and Deputy Attorney General James Comey threatened to resign if it continued. What exactly was the executive branch up to that caused so much dissent even among its own loyalists? Who was victimized during this time? Why are we not hearing the answers—or even the questions?

The misnamed Patriot Act, presented to the public as an antiterrorism measure, actually focuses on American citizens rather than foreign terrorists. The definition of "terrorism" for federal criminal purposes is greatly expanded, such that legitimate protest against the government could someday place an American under federal surveillance. Similarly, your Internet use can be monitored without your knowledge, and your Internet provider can be forced to hand over user information to law enforcement without a warrant or subpoena.

The biggest problem with these new law enforcement powers is that they bear little relationship to fighting terrorism. Surveillance powers are greatly expanded, and checks and balances on government are greatly reduced. "Sneak and peek" and blanket searches are becoming more frequent every day. Most of the provisions have been sought by domestic law enforcement agencies for years, not to fight terrorism but rather to increase their police power over the American people. The federal government has not shown us that it failed to detect or prevent the September 11 attacks because it lacked the powers over our lives that it was granted under the Patriot Act.

We now know that plenty of red flags that should have alerted officials to the hijackers' plot were ignored. That was a matter of government ineptness, not a lack of surveillance power. *Our officials had the evidence.* They simply failed to act on it. And they then turned around and exploited their own failure as an excuse to crack down on the American people, demanding new powers that would have done nothing to prevent 9/11. Only government could get away with such a transparent sham.

The Patriot Act violates the Constitution by allowing searches and seizures of American citizens and their property without a warrant issued by an independent court upon a finding of probable cause. Foreign Intelligence Surveillance Courts, whose standards do not meet the constitutional requirements of the Fourth Amendment, may issue warrants for individual records, including medical and library records. It can do so secretly, and the person who turns over the records is muzzled and cannot ever speak of the search. The attorney general is given the power, with no judicial oversight, to write "national security letters" ordering holders of any of your personal records to hand them over for the government to examine—a power that has already been abused. You would have no way of knowing that this had been done.

Requiring a showing of probable cause before a warrant may be issued would in no way hamper terrorist investigations. For one thing, federal authorities still have plenty of tools available to investigate and monitor the activities of noncitizens suspected of terrorism. Second, restoring Fourth Amendment protections would not interfere with those provisions of the Patriot Act that remove the firewalls that once prevented the government's law enforcement and intelligence agencies from sharing information.

The probable cause requirements will likewise not delay a terrorist investigation. Preparations can be made for the issuance of a warrant in the event of an emergency, and allowances can be made for cases in which law enforcement does not have time to obtain a warrant. In fact, a requirement that law enforcement demonstrate probable cause may help law enforcement officials focus their efforts on true threats, thereby avoiding the problem of information overload that is handicapping the government's efforts to identify sources of terrorist financing.

History demonstrates that the powers we give the federal government today will remain in place indefinitely. How sure are we that future presidents won't abuse those powers? Politically motivated IRS audits and FBI investigations have been used by past administrations to destroy political enemies. Past abuses of executive surveillance are the reason FISA was passed in the first place.

Even some of the most ardent supporters of the current wave of federal privacy violations and assaults on civil liberties once held—when Bill Clinton was calling for them, at least—that these powers were too dangerous to entrust to government. John Ashcroft, attorney general for several years during the Bush administration and a strong supporter of the Patriot Act, was not always so cavalier about civil liberties. While a U.S. senator during the Clinton years, Ashcroft warned about proposed invasions of privacy:

> The Clinton administration would like the federal government to have the capability to read any international or domestic computer communications. The FBI wants access to decode, digest, and discuss financial transactions, personal e-mail, and proprietary information sent abroad—all in the name of national security.
>
> The administration's interest in all e-mail is a wholly unhealthy precedent, especially given this administration's track record on FBI files and IRS snooping. Every medium by which people communicate can be subject to exploitation by those with illegal intentions. Nevertheless, this is no reason to hand Big Brother the keys to unlock our e-mail diaries, open our ATM records, read our medical records, or translate our international communications. . . . The implications here are far-reaching, with impacts that touch individual users, companies, libraries, universities, teachers, and students.

Here is an articulate statement of caution and skepticism. But a Republican administration calls for the same powers, and all these concerns go sailing out the window.

Other conservatives were just as wary of the surveillance powers requested by the Clinton administration, aware that they could easily be abused and employed for partisan or ideological purposes. For instance, "terrorism" could simply be defined as activism on behalf of a cause the current administration in Washington disapproved of. And as far back as the 1970s, the conservative scholar Robert Nisbet was cautioning:

The day is long past when this phrase ["national security"] was restricted to what is required in actual war. As everyone knows, it has been, since World War II under FDR, a constantly widening cloak or umbrella for governmental actions of every conceivable degree of power, stealth, and cunning by an ever-expanding corps of government officials. . . . As we now know in detail, the utilization of the FBI and other paramilitary agencies by Presidents and other high executive department officers for the purposes of eavesdropping, electronic bugging, and similarly intimate penetrations of individual privacy goes straight back to FDR, and the practice has only intensified and widened ever since. Naturally, all such royalist invasions have been justified, right down to Watergate, under the name of national security. The record is clear and detailed that national security cover-up has been a practice of each of the Presidents since FDR.

Judge Andrew Napolitano recently asked, "Why should government agents spy on us? They work for *us*. How about we spy on them? On cops when they arrest and interrogate people or contemplate suspending freedom; on prosecutors when they decide whom to prosecute and what evidence to use; on judges when they rationalize away our guaranteed rights; and on members of Congress whenever they meet with a lobbyist, mark up a piece of legislation, or conspire to assault or liberties or our pocketbooks."

For a patriotic American, there is nothing radical about this attitude at all. *This is how the Founding Fathers thought.* If our critics want to repudiate the Founding Fathers, let them go ahead and do it. If they won't be honest enough to do so, they should at least refrain from condemning those of us who still believe in the wisdom they left for posterity.

Much more is at stake here than privacy violations or unconstitutional searches, important and dangerous as those are. For example, the president has made clear, in one of his signing statements, that he retains the power to engage in torture regardless of congressional statutes to the contrary. Defense Department memoranda say the same thing.

First of all, legal issues aside, the American people and government should never abide the use of torture by our military or intelligence agencies. A decent society never accepts or justifies torture. It dehumanizes both torturer and victim, yet seldom produces reliable intelligence. Torture by rogue American troops or agents puts all Americans at risk, especially our rank-and-file soldiers stationed in dozens of dangerous places around the globe. It is not difficult to imagine American soldiers or travelers being taken hostage and tortured as some kind of sick retaliation for Abu Ghraib.

Beyond that is the threat posed by unchecked executive power. Executive branch lawyers claim that the president's commander-in-chief powers override federal laws prohibiting torture. But the argument for extraordinary wartime executive powers has been made time and again, always with bad results and the loss of our liberties. War has been used by presidents to excuse the imprisonment of American citizens of Japanese descent, to silence speech, to suspend habeas corpus, and even to control entire private industries. That's why it is precisely during times of relative crisis that we should adhere most closely to the Constitution, not abandon it. The Founders were especially concerned about the consolidation of power during times of war and national emergencies. War does not justify the suspension of torture laws any more than it justifies the suspension of murder laws, the suspension of due process, or the suspension of the Second Amendment.

The hallowed right of habeas corpus has also been a casualty of the war on terror. The Military Commissions Act of 2006 gives the president the power to detain people indefinitely and to deny the accused any real opportunity to answer the charges against them. It is anti-American at its core. The name of the Act can give the misleading impression that anyone targeted under it can at least bring his case before a military commission. That is not so. If the president wants to punish an accused "enemy combatant," he may bring him before such a commission. But he need not, and if he'd rather that the person remain in prison forever, he is free to adopt that course instead.

This legislation gave legal backing to practices in which the administration had already been engaged. Ali Saleh Kahlah al-Marri, a citizen of Qatar, married with five children, was living in America legally in 2001 when he was charged with making false statements in connection with the investigation of 9/11. He was slated to be tried in July 2003. Whatever the merits of the case against him, what happened next is an astonishing departure from American principles and tradition. Before the case could go to trial, the president suddenly declared al-Marri to be an "enemy combatant," whereupon the charges against him were dismissed by the civilian court and he was sent to a military prison, indefinitely.

We need to come to our senses: it cannot be tolerable for the president to have the right to detain people indefinitely, even for life, and not even permit them to review the charges against them.

The argument is not that criminals or terrorists should be let loose. Constitutionalists are merely saying that people are at least entitled to confront the charges against them.

The case of José Padilla is especially striking. We first heard that Padilla was planning to set off a radiological bomb (a "dirty bomb") in an American city. The government never wound up charging him with that offense, which it had wrung from him by torture. The charges it did finally bring against him were rather more vague and less interesting.

But the federal government did not bring charges against him right away. Instead, Padilla was declared an "enemy combatant," and therefore sent to prison indefinitely without any charges being brought against him. The only reason charges were finally brought against Padilla some three and a half years later is that the administration was afraid that the Supreme Court would rule against its treatment of him. By hearing his case, the administration could head off the Court by declaring that Padilla had received the trial he sought, and that his complaint was therefore moot.

During the three and a half years he was in custody, Padilla was made to endure various forms of torture. Kept in solitary confinement, Padilla was subjected to variations of sleep deprivation. Noxious fumes were introduced into his cell. His cell was made extremely cold for long periods of time. He was drugged, disoriented, and threatened with all manner of gruesome fates.

It is time for us to wake up. We have allowed the president to abduct an American citizen on American soil, declare him an "enemy combatant" (a charge the accused has no power to contest, which is rendered by the president in secret and is unreviewable), detain him indefinitely, deny him legal counsel, and subject him to inhumane treatment. How can we not be concerned about such a thing? Have we been so blinded by propaganda that we have forgotten basic American principles, and legal guarantees that extend back to our British forbears eight centuries ago? This is an outrageous offense against America and her Constitution. Claims that these powers will be exercised only against the bad guys are not worth listening to.

In April 2006, Pulitzer Prize–winning Associated Press photographer Bilal Hussein was detained by the American military in Iraq, joining at least 14,000 others around the world who have been similarly detained by the U.S. government. He was never charged with a crime, and demands for information from the Associated Press were met with stonewalling. The AP unsuccessfully demanded his release, or at least that formal charges be filed against him. (Hussein was finally released in April 2008.)

The AP was finally told that their photographer had been involved in the kidnapping of two journalists in Ramadi, but this story didn't hold water: the journalists in question said that Hussein had actually been very helpful to them after their release, when they had no car and no money. That unpersuasive story did nothing to remove the widespread suspicion that the real reason for the AP photographer's detention involved his photographs of the war zone, which were said to have displeased American officials.

What has happened to our country and its image around the world, and why are we allowing it?

In this book I have tried to make as few references to specific pieces of legislation as possible, because my preference is to focus on ideas rather than minutiae, and I have never had much interest in assembling a policy manual. I need to make an exception here, since a piece of legislation I introduced into Congress in late 2007 concisely reflects my views on civil liberties and executive power in light of the war on terror. I am referring to the American Freedom Agenda Act of 2007.

Among other things, the legislation

- repeals the Military Commissions Act of 2006;
- forbids the use of statements extracted by torture as evidence in any civilian of military tribunal;
- subordinates the executive's surveillance activities to the requirements of the Foreign Intelligence Surveillance Act (FISA);
- gives the House of Representatives and the Senate legal standing to contest in court any presidential signing statement that indicates the executive's intention to disregard any provision of a bill; and
- provides that nothing in the Espionage Act of 1917 prevents any journalist from publishing information received from the executive branch or Congress "unless the publication would cause direct, immediate, and irreparable harm to the national security of the United States."

Additionally, the legislation authorizes the president to establish military commissions for the prosecution of war crimes "only in places of active hostilities against the United States where an immediate trial is necessary to preserve fresh evidence or to prevent local anarchy." He is prohibited from "detaining any individual indefinitely as an unlawful enemy combatant absent proof by substantial evidence that the individual has directly engaged in active hostilities against the United States, provided that no United States citizen shall be detained as an unlawful enemy combatant." Any individual detained as an enemy combatant by the United States "shall be entitled to petition for a writ of habeas corpus under section 2241 of title 28, United States Code."

The Act also says, "No officer or agent of the United States shall kidnap, imprison, or torture any person abroad based solely on the President's belief that the subject of the kidnapping, imprisonment, or torture is a criminal or enemy combatant; provided that kidnapping shall be permitted if undertaken with the intent of bringing the kidnapped person for prosecution or interrogation to gather intelligence before a tribunal that meets international standards of fairness and due process." Knowing violations of this section are to be punished as felonies.

It amazes me that this kind of legislation should even be necessary in America. These are principles that Americans should insist their presidents not only observe, but actually believe in.

Those of us who still mention the Constitution, even now, and our obligation to observe it, are sometimes answered with the curt reply, "We're at war." We are indeed fighting undeclared wars in Iraq and Afghanistan, and an open-ended war against terrorism worldwide. But if the president claims extraordinary wartime powers, and we fight undeclared wars with no beginning and no end, when if ever will those extraordinary powers lapse? Since terrorism will never be eliminated completely, should all future presidents be able to act without regard to Congress or the Constitution simply by asserting "We're at war"?

Toward the end of 2007, Senator Jeff Sessions declared, "Some people in this chamber love the Constitution more than they love the safety of this nation. We should all send President Bush a letter thanking him for protecting us." What kind of sheep must politicians take Americans for if they expect us to fall for creepy propaganda like this?

The war on terror, therefore, has had dangerous and undesirable domestic consequences. So has the war on drugs. Saying so doesn't win any popularity contests: people's opinions on this issue are so deeply and fervently held that it can be very difficult to persuade them to revisit the evidence dispassionately.

But revisit it we must. We seriously mistake the function of government if we think its job is to regulate bad habits or supplant the role of all those subsidiary bodies in society that have responsibility for forming our moral character. Our misplaced confidence in government has once again had exceedingly unpleasant results. "A barrage of research and opinion," writes economist Dan Klein, "has pounded [the drug war] for being the cause of increased street crime, gang activity, drug adulteration, police corruption, congested courts and overcrowded jails. Drug prohibition creates a black-market combat zone that society cannot control."

The drug war has wrought particular devastation in minority neighborhoods, as decent parents find themselves consistently undermined when they try to teach good values to their children. When the lucrative profits from the black market in drugs make drug dealers the most ostentatiously prosperous sector of society, it is much more difficult for parents to persuade their children to shun those profits and pursue a much less remunerative, if more honorable, line of work. Putting an end to the federal drug war would immediately pull the rug out from under the drug lords who have unleashed a reign of terror over our cities. Finally, the good Americans who live there could make their homes livable once again.

Although many conservatives support the federal war on drugs, an increasing number, like William F. Buckley, are skeptical. The conservative economist Thomas Sowell finds the whole thing more utopian than conservative: "What would make still more sense [than the current policy] would be to admit that we are not God, that we cannot live other people's lives or save people who don't want to be saved, and to take the profits out of drugs by decriminalizing them. That is what destroyed the bootleggers' gangs after Prohibition was repealed."

This is not an unusual perspective in the Christian tradition as well. In the Treatise on Law in his *Summa Theologica*, Thomas Aquinas explains (citing Augustine) that not all vices should be punished by the law. Human laws should chiefly forbid those things that cause direct physical harm to others; Aquinas offers murder and theft as examples. With regard to practices that do not physically harm or defraud others (whatever other intangible grief they may cause), it can be necessary to tolerate them if prohibiting them would lead to still further evils—a point that is especially relevant to our subject here.

What is more, the law cannot make a wicked person virtuous. According to Aquinas, God's grace alone can accomplish such a thing. The law is simply incompetent here. What the law can do is provide the peace and order within which men can conduct their affairs. But so much of what is important in human life takes place far removed from law, and in the domain of civil society, families, and communities. These salutary influences, apart from the state, have a responsibility to improve the moral conduct of individuals. We ought not to shirk our own responsibility by looking to politicians—who are not exactly known for living beyond moral reproach themselves—to carry out so important a function.

When you actually study the beginnings of the federal war on drugs, you uncover a history of lies, bigotry, and ignorance so extensive it will leave you speechless.

In one area, at least, those who had favored the prohibition of alcoholic beverages had been honest: the Constitution does not authorize the federal government simply to ban these substances. When alcohol prohibition was implemented, everyone understood that it required a constitutional amendment. And so in order to ban certain kinds of drugs, the Harrison Tax Act of 1914 simply levied prohibitively high taxes on them. No one would pay such high taxes, so anyone caught in possession of the substances targeted by the act was accused not of mere possession, which was not criminalized, but of tax evasion.

Here I intend to focus on the especially interesting history of federal marijuana prohibition. A substantial motivation behind it, which is evident all over the debates on the subject, was a contempt for Mexicans, with whom marijuana use was widely associated at the time. On the floor of the Texas Senate, one state senator declared: "All Mexicans are crazy, and this stuff is what makes them crazy." Similar statements could be heard in numerous states around the country. Harry Anslinger, who headed the federal government's Bureau of Narcotics, said that "the primary reason to outlaw marijuana is its effect on the degenerate races." That was not unusual: Anslinger made comments like that as a matter of routine.

The resulting Marijuana Tax Act of 1937—yes, federal prohibition is really just seven decades old—had little to do with real science or medicine, and a lot to do with petty ethnic grudges, careerism in the Bureau of Narcotics, and disinformation and propaganda in the popular press, where yellow journalism still lived. Hearings on this important matter took a grand total of two hours, very little of which had anything to do with the health effects of marijuana, the alleged reason behind the proposed prohibition.*

A grand total of two medical experts testified on the subject. One alleged expert was James Munch, a professor who claimed to have injected 300 dogs with the active ingredient in marijuana, and that two had died. When asked whether he had chosen dogs for the similarity of their reactions to those of human beings, he shrugged, "I wouldn't know; I am not a dog psychologist."

We can be fairly certain that this professor had not injected these dogs with the active ingredient in marijuana, since that ingredient was synthesized for the first time in a laboratory in Holland years later. But keep this gentleman in mind for a moment.

The other expert who testified was William Woodward, who represented the American Medical Association. He denounced the legislation as medically unsound and the product of ignorance and propaganda. "The American Medical Association knows of

---

*I am indebted for much of this discussion to Charles Whitebread and Richard Bonnie, *Marihuana Conviction: The Legal History of Drugs in the United States* (Charlottesville: University of Virginia Press, 1974).

no evidence that marihuana is a dangerous drug," he said. To which one congressman replied, "Doctor, if you can't say anything good about what we are trying to do, why don't you go home?"

In Congress, the entire debate on national marijuana prohibition took about a minute and a half.

"Mr. Speaker, what is this bill about?" asked a congressman from New York.

"I don't know," came the reply. "It has something to do with a thing called marihuana. I think it's a narcotic of some kind."

Then a second question from the congressman: "Mr. Speaker, does the American Medical Association support this bill?"

The AMA opposed the bill, as we've seen. But the Speaker replied, "Their Doctor Wentworth [sic] came down here. They support this bill 100 percent."

And with that untruth ended the entire congressional debate on the prohibition policy.

After the 1937 legislation was passed, Anslinger held a major national conference to which he invited everyone he could find who knew something about marijuana. Of the 42 people invited, 39 stood up at the event and more or less said they didn't understand why they had been asked to come, and that they knew nothing about the subject. That left three people: (1) the AMA's William Woodward, (2) Dr. Woodward's assistant, and (3) James Munch, the professor with the dogs.

You can guess what happened next. James Munch, the one person at the conference who agreed with Anslinger on marijuana, was named the Official Expert on marijuana at the Federal Bureau of Narcotics. One person agrees with the government's position and he is appointed the Official Expert. If that doesn't sum up how government operates, I don't know what does.

Now recall Anslinger's claim—which he later withdrew in the face of the medical community's insistence that there was no evidence to support it—that marijuana "is an addictive drug which produces in its users insanity, criminality, and death." In the late 1930s and early 1940s, defendants in a series of well-publicized murder trials happily exploited that statement by offering—what else?—insanity defenses on the grounds that they had used the drug prior to committing the crime.

At one of these trials our Official Expert was asked to testify about the substance's insanity-inducing properties. In his testimony in a Newark, New Jersey, court Munch admitted to having used the drug himself. When asked what had happened when he had used the drug, he answered: "After two puffs on a marijuana cigarette, I was turned into a bat."

As a bat he flew around the room for fifteen minutes, he said.

Naturally, this was all the defense needed to hear. Accused murderers in that trial now testified, "After two puffs on a marijuana cigarette my incisor teeth grew six inches long and dripped with blood." All marijuana insanity defenses were successful.

Meanwhile, Anslinger informed Munch that his position as Official Expert would be jeopardized if he continued to testify that he had become a bat. He stopped testifying.

By 1970, the federal government dropped the charade that this was all a tax measure and simply prohibited a range of substances. No constitutional justification for this new prohibition has been offered.

We do not treat alcoholics as criminals and throw them in prison. Politicians enjoy drinking alcohol, after all, so that would never happen. In the same way, drug abuse is a medical problem, not a problem for courts and policemen. Families, churches, and communities need to take responsibility when people harm their lives with drugs. Clogging our courts and prisons with cases involving people found in possession of tiny quantities of prohibited substances, and who have never done any physical harm to anyone, makes it all but impossible to devote the necessary resources to tracking down the violent criminals who really do threaten us. Over the past two decades more people have been imprisoned on drug offenses than for all violent crimes put together. And that is not to mention the continued erosion of our civil liberties for which the drug war has been responsible.

The failure of the federal war on drugs should be clear enough from one simple fact: our government has been unable to keep drugs even out of prisons, which are surrounded by armed guards. The fact is, drugs are already available to people who want them. That is the nightmare scenario that people fear, but they fail to realize that we are already there. Poll after poll finds the vast bulk of high school and college students easily able to acquire drugs if they so desire. That is how black markets work: prohibiting something that is highly desired does not make the desire go away but merely ensures that the supply of that good is provided in the most dangerous and undesirable manner possible, and endows criminal sectors of society with additional wealth and power. As with so much else, the constitutional solution would get the federal government out of the picture and leave the issue to the states.

Regardless of where one stands on the broader drug war, we should all be able to agree on the subject of medical marijuana. Here, the use of an otherwise prohibited substance has been found to relieve unbearable suffering in countless patients. How can we fail to support liberty and individual responsibility in such a clear-cut case? What harm does it do to anyone else to allow fellow human beings in pain to find the relief they need? What kind of "compassionate conservatism" is this?

As usual, this constitutional outrage enjoys bipartisan support. The Clinton administration issued threats against states that permitted medical marijuana, warning that it would bring charges against any physician who prescribed it. In 2005, Clinton Supreme Court appointees Ruth Bader Ginsburg and Stephen Breyer both upheld the federal government's alleged power to prohibit medical marijuana even in the dozen states like California that had voted to allow it. (Alabama, Mississippi, and Louisiana, which do not allow medical marijuana and have tough drug laws, issued a joint statement saying that although they opposed California's policy, they were even more strongly opposed to a federal government that could overturn that policy and in effect make up its powers as it went along.)

The constitutional arguments in favor of allowing the federal government to prosecute medical marijuana users even in states in which ballot initiatives have made the practice legal are an insult to the American people. They are based on a complete misunderstanding of the Constitution's commerce clause and what its scope was supposed to be. On the other hand, if you'd like to see how the issue is dealt with by someone who actually cares to consider the original intent of the Constitution, then treat yourself to Justice Clarence Thomas's eloquent dissent in *Gonzales v. Raich* (2005).

———

The personal liberties that concern me extend beyond individuals and include families and households as well. For one thing, I have always supported homeschooling families, who run the ideological gamut from Vermont environmentalists to Southern evangelicals. As I have said, the government does not own you— and neither does it own your children. It is bad enough that some parents find themselves forced to pay for an education they not only will not use for their children, but whose content they deeply oppose from a philosophical or religious point of view. (I've sometimes wondered why those who would never dream of forcibly taking people's money to pay to support a religious belief they do not share have no hesitation at all in taking their money to support an educational philosophy they do not share.) It is even worse that in some cases they have to maneuver a legal minefield in order to provide their children with the kind of education they want.

One could write a lengthy book on the ways in which government intrudes upon the legitimate rights of the family, but consider this example, which is all the more interesting for having been ignored in the media. In 2004, a presidential initiative called the New Freedom Commission on Mental Health issued a report calling for forced mental health screening for all American children, beginning in preschool. Although no such program has begun at the federal level, grants have already been sent out to establish pilot programs in localities across the country in conformity with the New Freedom report. I think we know what that means.

Before considering just how outrageous this proposal is, let us consider the obvious beneficiary of such a program: the pharmaceutical industry. There can be little doubt that under such a program, millions more children would suddenly be discovered to be in need of psychotropic drugs. Some 2.5 million American children use such drugs already, with (according to the *Journal of the American Medical Association*) a 300 percent increase from 1991 through 1995 alone. The figure increased another fivefold from 1995 to 2002.

Is this a good thing? We have reason to be skeptical. We have no idea what the long-term side effects of the use of such drugs in children, whose brains are still developing, will be. Medical science has not even exhaustively identified every possible brain chemical, even as we alter youngsters' brains with drugs. Short-term side effects are already apparent in many children, yet parents have actually been threatened with child-abuse charges if they refuse to drug their children. It will be all the more difficult to resist such a regimen if a federal mental-health screener recommends it. Diagnoses of some of these disorders are notoriously subjective; and physician Karen Effrem wonders if children could even be stigmatized simply for having religious or political views that differ from fashionable orthodoxies.

The key question, though, is by what right government intrudes into such an area. The issue of mental health is obviously a question for parents, children, and their doctors to deal with themselves. What kind of free people would turn their children's most intimate health matters over to government strangers?

Ever since this report appeared I have sought to deny funding to any such program. My opponents have described this as an overreaction. But in light of how our government normally behaves, is it really? If the history of American government teaches us anything, it is that the time to fight oppressive and absurd programs is *before they are established*, since once they are in place they are essentially impossible to dismantle. They need to be blocked before they have a chance to start. Otherwise, local programs with federal funding will grow larger and larger and be found in many more localities, until we finally have a mandatory federal screening program. This is how it always works.

I mention this example not because it is the most pressing issue facing our republic today but simply because it is so revealing: a report commissioned by the executive branch casually recommends mandatory mental-health screening of all American children, and it receives next to no attention. Even a generation ago the media would have picked up on this, and American parents would have rejected it so contemptuously that no one would have dared to bring it up again. This program is also a useful object lesson in how assaults on our liberties sometimes begin— limited in scope and full of benign language—and how special interests, in this case the psychiatric establishment and the pharmaceutical industry, adopt the line that they're just looking out for the common good. (I am sure it is just a coincidence that thanks to the proposal they will happen to get millions of additional clients for free.)

Our Constitution was written to restrain government, not the people. Government is always tempted to turn that maxim upside down. Little wonder that George Washington, the father of our country, once said, "Government is not reason; it is not eloquent; it is force. Like fire, it is a dangerous servant and a fearful master."

CHAPTER 6

Money: The Forbidden Issue in American Politics

Americans are concerned about our financial picture: the housing bubble, the collapsing dollar, the specter of inflation. Most don't know what's causing it, but they correctly sense that something in our economic system is rotten.

Neither political party will speak to them frankly and honestly. Instead, the people are told by the talking heads on television that their rulers know just what is wrong and will promptly put things right. A little more monetary manipulation by the Federal Reserve is all the economy needs, and there is nothing fundamentally wrong with the system.

These contrived, self-serving answers satisfy very few, but they are all the answers the American people are ever given.

Once again, Americans are deprived of a full and fruitful debate on a subject of the utmost importance. The entire range of debate is limited to minor tinkering: should the Fed make this trivial adjustment or that one? Read the major newspapers and watch the cable news channels: you will not see any fundamental questions raised. The debate will be resolutely confined to superficialities.

In the year 2000, I wrote: "The relative soundness of our currency that we enjoy as we move into the twenty-first century will not persist. The instability in world currency markets, because of the dollar's acceptance for so many years as a reserve currency, will cause devastating adjustments that Congress will eventually be forced to deal with." As 2007 and 2008 wore on, the precipitous decline of the dollar dramatically undercut all the promises and assurances that the system was just fine. It wasn't.

More half-measures will only prolong the inevitable day of reckoning. It is long past time for Americans to look beyond the snake oil salesmen whose monetary system has destroyed the value of our dollar and seek wisdom instead from the free-market economists who spent much of the twentieth century warning about exactly the kind of money we have right now. The more knowledge the American people have, the more likely is our return to a sensible monetary system. As John Adams wrote to Thomas Jefferson in 1787, "All the perplexities, confusions, and distress in America, arise, not from defects in their Constitution or Confederation, not from a want of honor or virtue, so much as from downright ignorance of the nature of coin, credit, and circulation."

The Constitution is clear about the monetary powers of the federal government. Congress has a constitutional responsibility to maintain the value of the dollar by making only gold and silver legal tender and not to "emit bills of credit." The records from the Founders make perfectly clear that that was their intention. The power to regulate the value of money does not mean the federal government can debase the currency; the Framers would never have given the federal government such a power. It is nothing more than a power to codify an already existing definition of the dollar (which antedated the Constitution) in terms of gold; it also refers to the government's power to declare the ratio between gold and silver, or gold and any other metal, based on the market values of those metals.

This responsibility was carried out relatively well in the nineteenth century, despite the abuse the dollar suffered during the Civil War and despite repeated efforts to form a central bank. This policy served to maintain relatively stable prices, and problems arose only when the rules of the gold standard were ignored or abused. (Superficial economic histories of the nineteenth century blame economic hard times, absurdly enough, on the gold standard; a good antidote is Murray N. Rothbard's *A History of Money and Banking in the United States: The Colonial Era to World War II*.)

The Founding Fathers had had plenty of experience with paper money, and it turned the great majority of them firmly against it. The Revolutionary War was financed in part by the government-issued Continental currency, which was not backed by gold, which people were forced to use, and which the government issued in greater and greater abundance until its value was completely destroyed. Little wonder that most American statesmen opposed the issuance of paper money by the government, and the Constitution they drafted nowhere granted the federal government such a power.

For that reason, James Madison once wrote that the constitutional prohibition of bills of credit (what we would understand as paper money) should

give pleasure to every citizen in proportion to his love of justice and his knowledge of the true springs of public prosperity. The loss which America has sustained since the peace, from the pestilent effects of paper money on the necessary confidence between man and man, on the necessary confidence in the public councils, on the industry and morals of the people, and on the character of republican government, constitutes an enormous debt against the States chargeable with this unadvised measure.

Throughout most of American history the dollar has been defined as a specific weight in gold. Until 1933, in fact, 20 dollars could be redeemed for one ounce of gold. But that year, the U.S. government went off the gold standard, and henceforth American currency would be redeemable into nothing. The government actually confiscated Americans' holdings of monetary gold, nullified even private contracts that called for payment for a good or service in gold, and declared the dollar no longer redeemable into gold by American citizens—but made allowances for redemption by foreign central banks at 35 dollars an ounce, a devaluation of the dollar from its previous ratio of $20.67 an ounce. And even this tenuous link to gold was severed in 1971, when Richard Nixon declared that within a year, at the $35 exchange rate, we would not have an ounce of gold remaining. Other governments had begun to realize that the dollar, which was being massively inflated, was losing its value, and more and more were demanding gold in exchange for dollars. At that point Nixon officially closed the gold window, so that not even foreign central banks could get gold for dollars. In so doing, he cut the dollar's last lingering tie to gold.

Now let's consider at least a few of the nuts and bolts of how the Federal Reserve System typically operates. When we read that the Federal Reserve chairman is cutting interest rates, what does that mean? Analysts are referring to something called the federal funds rate, the rate that banks charge when they borrow from each other. The banks are required to keep a specific fraction of their deposits on reserve, as opposed to lent out, to be available for customer withdrawal. Banks can find themselves below the re-serve requirement set by the Fed if they have made a lot of loans or if an unusually large number of people have withdrawn funds. Banks borrow from each other when they need additional cash reserves to meet the reserve requirement.

The federal funds rate rises when there is too much demand from banks looking to borrow and too little supply from banks willing to lend. For reasons we shall see in a moment, the Fed often wants to prevent the federal funds rate from rising. Al-though it cannot directly set the rate, it can intervene in the economy in such a way as to push it upward or downward. The way it pushes the rate down is by buying bonds from the banks. That gives the banks more money and therefore more reserves on hand to lend to banks that need it. Funds available to be lent to other banks are now less scarce, and a correspondingly lower federal funds rate reflects this.

Where does the Fed get the money to buy the bonds? It creates it out of thin air, simply writing checks on itself and giving them to banks. If that sounds fishy, then you understand it just fine.

Here, finally, is how the Fed's activity leads to lower interest rates offered by banks. Thanks to Fed purchases of bonds from the banks, the banks now have excess reserves they can lend (ei-ther to other banks or to individuals or corporations). In order to attract additional borrowers, though, they must lower their interest rates, reduce their lending standards, or both.

When the Fed intervenes like this, increasing the money supply with money and credit it creates out of thin air, it causes all kinds of economic problems. It decreases the value of the dollar, thereby making people poorer. And in the long run even the apparent stimulus to the economy that comes from all the additional borrowing and spending turns out to be harmful as well, for this phony prosperity actually sows the seeds for hard times and recession down the road.

First, consider the effects of inflation, by which we mean the Fed's increase in the supply of money, on the value of the dollar. By increasing the supply of money, the Federal Reserve lowers the value of every dollar that already exists. If the supply of Mickey Mantle baseball cards were suddenly to increase a millionfold, each individual card would become almost valueless. The same principle applies to money: the more the Fed creates, the less value each individual monetary unit possesses. When the money supply is increased, prices rise—with each dollar now worth less than before, it can purchase fewer goods than it could in the past. Or imagine an art auction in which bidders are each given an additional million dollars. Would we not expect bids to go up? The market works the same way, except in a free market there are numerous sellers instead of the one seller in an auction.

All right, some may say, prices may indeed rise, but so do wages and salaries, and therefore inflation causes no real problems on net. This misconception overlooks one of the most insidious and immoral effects of inflation: its redistribution of wealth from the poor and middle class to the politically well connected. The price increases that take place as a result of inflation do not occur all at once and to the same degree. Those who receive the new money first receive it before prices have yet risen. They enjoy a windfall. Meanwhile, as they spend the new money, and the next wave of recipients spend it, and so on, prices begin to rise throughout the economy—well before the new money has trickled down to most people. The average person is now paying higher prices while still earning his old income, which has not yet been adjusted to account for the higher money supply. By the time the new money has made its way throughout the economy, average people have all this time been paying higher prices, and only now can begin to break even. The enrichment of the politically well connected—in other words, those who get the newly created money first: government contractors, big banks, and the like—comes at the direct expense of everyone else. These are known as the distribution effects, or Cantillon effects, of inflation, after economist Richard Cantillon. The average person is silently robbed through this invisible means and usually doesn't understand what exactly is happening to him. And almost no one in the political establishment has an incentive to tell him.

I have already discussed health care, but it's important to understand that rising health care costs cannot be understood apart from the money question. With government so heavily involved in medicine, that is where so much of the new money is directed. Thus health costs tend to rise faster than other costs because of the distribution effects of inflation: wherever government spends its new money, that is where higher prices will be most immediate and evident.

When the value of Americans' savings is deliberately eroded through inflation, that is a tax, albeit a hidden one. I call it the inflation tax, a tax that is all the more insidious for being so underhanded: most Americans have no idea what causes it or why their standard of living is going down. Meanwhile, government and its favored constituencies receive their ill-gotten loot. The racket is safe as long as no one figures out what is going on.

Incidentally, wise Americans from our nation's past understood the damage that unbacked paper money could do to society's most vulnerable. "The rise of prices that follows an expansion of [paper money]," wrote William Gouge, Andrew Jackson's Treasury adviser, "does not affect all descriptions of labor and commodities, at the same time, to an equal degree. . . . Wages appear to be among the last things that are raised. . . . The working man finds all the articles he uses in his family rising in price, while the money rate of his own wages remains the same." Jackson himself warned that an inflationary monetary policy by means of "spurious paper currency" is "always attended by a loss to the laboring classes." Likewise, Senator Daniel Webster maintained that "of all the contrivances for cheating the laboring classes of mankind, none has been found more effectual than that which deludes them with paper money."

Moreover, the "inflation rate" itself, which is tracked using the Consumer Price Index (CPI), tends to be measured in a misleading way. Ask the average American if he thinks prices are going up by only a few percent per year, as the official figures would have it. So-called core inflation figures do not include food or energy, whose prices have been rising rapidly.

But there is another, more significant way in which these kinds of measurements of "inflation" are designed to obscure rather than reveal. Ludwig von Mises used to say that governments will always try to get people to focus on prices when thinking about inflation. But rising prices are a *result* of inflation, not inflation itself. Inflation is the increase in the money supply. If we understood inflation that way, we would instantly know how to cure it: simply demand that the Federal Reserve cease increasing the money supply. By focusing our attention on prices instead, we are liable to misdiagnose the problem, and we are more apt to accept bogus government "solutions" like wage and price controls, as in the 1970s.

Let's now consider what really happens when the Fed lowers interest rates. We often hear calls for the Fed to do just that, as if forcing rates down were a costless way to bring about permanent prosperity. The alleged prosperity it brings about is neither costless nor permanent. When the Fed artificially lowers rates, it misrepresents economic conditions and misleads people into making unsound investments. Investments that would not have been profitable beforehand suddenly seem attractive in light of the lower interest rates. These are *malinvestments*, which would not have been undertaken if the business world had been able to view the economy clearly instead of being misled by the Fed's false signals.

In the short run, a false prosperity takes root. Business expands. New construction is everywhere. People feel wealthier. This is why there is always such political pressure on the Fed to lower rates around election time: the prosperity comes in the short run, and the painful correction comes much later, well after people have cast their votes.

As these borrowers spend the money they borrowed and compete with each other for resources, the result is a rise in prices and interest rates. This is how the economy reveals that more long-term projects have been begun than can be sustained in light of current resource availability. Some of them have to be abandoned, with all the dislocation that entails: layoffs, squandered capital, misdirected resources, and so on.

Interest rates were at their initial level for a reason: savings were low, and therefore with little for investors to borrow, the price of borrowing (i.e., the interest rate) was high. Had market-determined interest rates prevailed, investors would have been discouraged from excessive borrowing to finance long-term projects, and the result would have been sustainable investment and growth. Interest rates set by the market coordinate the production process in accordance with real economic conditions. Only the most profitable, socially demanded projects would have been undertaken. When the Federal Reserve artificially lowers rates, on the other hand, it systematically misleads investors and encourages unsustainable economic booms. F. A. Hayek's Nobel Prize in economics, which was awarded to him in 1974, had to do with exactly this: showing how central bank manipulation of interest rates and money cause havoc throughout the economy, and set the stage for an inevitable bust.

The Fed often tries to delay the day of reckoning, the painful period when the malinvestments are liquidated and the economy is restored to true health. It will cut rates yet again. The false prosperity continues, but the problem of malinvestment only gets worse. The Fed cannot carry on the charade forever: if it inflates without end, it risks hyperinflation and the destruction of the currency. In some cases, central banks find, after resorting time and again to inflation as a way of encouraging economic activity, that their policies no longer have any discernible effect. The system is simply exhausted.

The Japanese economy provides a vivid example of the futility of manipulating interest rates. Japan was in the economic doldrums throughout the 1990s despite its central bank's rate cuts. Ultimately, interest rates were cut to *zero*, where they remained for several years. The rate-cutting failed to stimulate the economy. Prosperity cannot be created out of thin air by a central bank.

This is one reason I was delighted to learn that comedian Jon Stewart, when he had former Fed chairman Alan Greenspan on his program, asked him why we needed a Federal Reserve, and why interest rates couldn't simply be set freely on the market. That was a great question, the sort of question noncomedians in America never seem to ask, and Greenspan sputtered around for a response. Even Greenspan supporters were shocked to observe how poorly he responded to a simple question about the very purpose of the institution he headed for nearly two decades.

Central economic planning has been as discredited as any idea can possibly be. But even though we point to our devotion to the free market, at the same time we centrally plan our monetary system, the very heart of the economy. Americans must reject the notion that one man, whether Alan Greenspan, Ben Bernanke, or any other chairman of the Federal Reserve Board, can know what the proper money supply and interest rates ought to be. Only the market can determine that. Americans must learn this lesson if we want to avoid continuous and deeper recessions and to get the economy growing in a healthy and sustainable fashion.

Few Americans during his tenure knew that Greenspan had once been an outspoken advocate of the gold standard as the only monetary system that a free society should consider. Not long after my return to Congress in the election of 1996, I spoke with Greenspan at a special event that took place just before he was to speak in front of the House Banking Committee. At this event congressmen had a chance to meet and have their pictures taken with the Fed chairman. I decided to bring along my original copy of his 1966 article from the *Objectivist Newsletter* called "Gold and Economic Freedom," an outstanding piece in which he laid out the economic and moral case for a commodity-based monetary system as against a fiat paper system. He graciously agreed to sign it for me. As he was doing so, I asked if he wanted to write a disclaimer on the article. He replied good-naturedly that he had recently reread the piece and that he would not change a word of it. I found that fascinating: could it be that, in his heart of hearts, Greenspan still believed in the bulletproof logic of that classic article?

Shortly afterward, I decided—perhaps a bit mischievously—to bring up that article and the arguments raised in it during a subsequent Greenspan appearance before the Committee. But the Federal Reserve Chairman was less sympathetic to those arguments when I raised the subject out in the open. He replied that his views had changed since that article was written, and he even advanced the preposterous assertion that the Fed did not facilitate government expansion and deficit spending.

Greenspan's real views, however interesting as a piece of trivia, are ultimately unimportant. It is the system itself that matters. In the same way, it is absurd for the Fed chairman to come to Congress and complain that the real problems in the economy stem from deficit spending and that it is solely Congress and its recklessness with the budget that is at fault. That is not so: it is the *entire system* that is to blame. Congress could not get away with spending beyond our means year after year if we did not have a Federal Reserve System ready to finance it all by purchasing bonds with money it creates out of thin air.

What the issue boils down to is: do we want a monetary system that politicians can manipulate to their advantage? Do we want them to have the ability to pay for all their extravagance by printing the money they need, thereby imposing a hidden tax on all Americans by eroding the value of our dollar?

Gold cannot be mined as cheaply as Federal Reserve notes can be printed. Nor can its supply be manipulated on a daily basis. There is a great dispersion of power in a gold standard system. That is the strength of the system, for it allows the people to check any monetary excesses of their rulers and does not allow the rulers to exploit the people by debasing the money.

The gold standard has historically been a bulwark against inflation. It is politically manipulated money such as we have had since the 1930s that causes our inflation. That should not be unexpected, or difficult to understand. The supply of gold is relatively fixed and grows only modestly. But in a free economy, capital investment leads to ever-greater productivity, and the ability to produce more and more goods over time. So with gold relatively stable on the one hand and the supply of goods growing by leaps and bounds on the other, the gold will tend to be worth more and more, and the prices of these goods will be lower and lower.

History bears this out. An item that cost $100 in 1913 (when the Federal Reserve Act was passed) would cost $2014.81 in 2006. An item that cost $100 in 2006 would have cost $4.96 in 1913. As we can see, the dollar has lost nearly all its value since the Fed was established. Now, if the gold standard had brought about such an outcome, we would never hear the end of all the howls of outrage. But the Fed does it and . . . utter silence. The Fed has managed to insulate itself from the kind of criticism that is normally directed at all other institutions that harm Americans.

And in fact the gold standard did no such thing. People's money increased in value under the gold standard. They were not looted by inflation. An item that cost $100 in 1820 would have cost only $63.02 in 1913.

The Federal Reserve now no longer reports the figures on M3, the total money supply. Spokesmen claim that among the reasons for this change is that it costs too much money to gather these figures—this from an institution that creates however much money it wants, is off the books, and is never audited. To the contrary, the real reason we don't get these figures anymore, I am certain, is that they are too revealing. They tell us more about what the Fed has been up to and the damage it has been doing to our dollar than they care for us to know.

Any government that inflates the money supply runs the risk of hyperinflation, which occurs when the money supply is increased so much as to render the currency completely worthless. It can occur very quickly and suddenly, and has a very rapid snowballing effect.

The textbook case in the twentieth century took place in Germany in 1923 (although a worse hyperinflation occurred in Hungary after World War II). When in that year the French occupied the Ruhr Valley, an industrial and resource-rich part of western Germany, the German government encouraged workers there to go on a general strike and refuse to work. It paid their salaries during that strike by simply printing the necessary money.

But the process spun out of the government's control. People could see their money was losing value. They knew that the longer they held it, the less it would buy. So they rushed out to buy anything they could, since just about anything was worth more than the valueless pieces of paper that German marks were rapidly becoming. And the more they spent, the higher prices rose, leading still more people to unload their currency on whatever was for sale in anticipation of still higher prices in the future. The result was the complete ruin of the German mark, which German children began gluing together to make kites and German adults burned in order to keep warm.

Who can be surprised to learn that it was also in 1923 that Adolf Hitler made his first attempt to seize power? Intolerance and extremism always find a readier audience in unfavorable or (as in this case) chaotic economic times.

In the United States, November 2007 alone saw wholesale prices increase by 3.2 percent—an annualized rate of nearly 40 percent. With all manner of bailouts contemplated for mortgage lenders and a Federal Reserve committed to ever more money creation, are we so sure that hyperinflation could not occur here? In fact, that outcome becomes more likely every day.

———

Inflation of the money supply also produces financial bubbles and instability. The monetary inflation of the 1990s helped yield $145 billion in profits for the NASDAQ companies between 1996 and 2000. That entire amount was then lost in a single year—not to mention the trillions of dollars of paper losses in stock values from their peak in early 2000. Politicians are all tears and pity about large stock-market losses, but they never make a connection between the bubble economy and the monetary inflation generated by the Federal Reserve. Congress has chosen instead to blame the analysts for misleading investors—a drop in the bucket compared to the misleading information for which the Federal Reserve has been responsible, what with the artificially low interest rates it has brought about and a financial market made flush with generous new credit at every sign of a correction over the past ten years. By preventing the liquidation of bad debt and the elimination of malinvestment and overcapacity, the Federal Reserve's actions help keep financial bubbles inflated and make the eventual collapse all the more severe.

It is this, the Fed's policy of artificially cheap credit, that caused the housing bubble that has caused so many Americans so much grief. Banks, awash in reserves created out of thin air by the Fed, began making mortgage loans to just about anyone. With credit freely available, people bought larger and more expensive homes than would otherwise have made sense. They were set up for disaster, when reality would inevitably reassert itself amid the fantasy world the Fed had created. Using Money Zero Maturity figures, we find that the increase in mortgage debt since the 2001 recession is equal to the Fed's increase in the money supply. That is where the new money went, and it is where the housing bubble came from.

And it wasn't just that people were enticed by all the available credit into living beyond their means. The housing bubble caused them to make other destructive and unwise decisions as well. With real estate prices artificially inflated, people felt wealthier. In light of how wealthy the value of their homes made them feel, they saved less. And as economist Mark Thornton puts it, Americans began using their homes as giant ATMs to withdraw cash from the equity they had built up.

The 1990s witnessed a dramatic upward trend in new housing starts. Revealingly, no downturn in housing starts was observed during the 2001 recession, the only recession on record in which no such downturn has taken place.

Few Americans will be surprised at the statistics: between 1998 and 2005, home prices increased by 45 percent. As Thornton points out, that figure is all the more remarkable when we remember all the forces that were simultaneously putting downward pressure on home prices, including new home-building technology, an increased supply of lower-priced labor, mainly from Mexico, and the fact that new housing tends to be built on lower-priced land. That prices could nevertheless rise so sharply is a sign of the severity of the bubble.

All this has real consequences for real people. As the bubble bursts, many will face foreclosure or bankruptcy and will see their credit ratings decimated. Construction firms will face hard times, and unemployment in the industry will rise sharply. The effects on the wider economy could be equally devastating.

In the midst of this disaster, where are those who will point the finger where it belongs? Who will call the Federal Reserve to account for injecting into the economy all the funny money that created the housing bubble in the first place?

Former Fed chairman Alan Greenspan once boasted that the Fed's policy had helped many more people buy homes. Those boasts became scarcer as the bubble began to burst and people's lives were thrown into turmoil. Government intervention always has unintended consequences that cause harm, a truism that applies just as strongly to interventions into the monetary system. Devastated homeowners are only the latest victims.

All kinds of easy options were available to just about anyone with any creditworthiness, including tiny or no down payments and adjustable-rate or interest-only mortgages. People who wanted to follow a more traditional path to homeownership, such as a fixed-rate mortgage and a 20 percent down payment, were completely shut out of this housing market, yet another perverse effect of the bubble.

———

So what should be done?

First of all, it's long past time to put the monetary issue back on the table as a subject for genuine discussion, and then to start asking some forbidden questions. For over a hundred years, the money issue has been absent from our political process. No political campaign has focused on it or even said much of anything about it. For most people, in fact, the Fed is a complete mystery, its operations incomprehensible. That seems to be just the way the Fed likes it. We are supposed to be bored by it. We are supposed to treat it as a given, like the air we breathe. We are supposed to have confidence in it—surely the experts who run our monetary system for us (and who of course have a vested interest in perpetuating the system we now have) couldn't be giving us bad advice! But point to it as the source of our eroding standard of living, the ravages of the boom-bust business cycle, and the financial bubbles that have ruined countless Americans? That is simply not to be found anywhere along the spectrum of allowable opinion in America.

It's time for some fresh thinking for a change—an unbiased, rational reappraisal of a monetary system that is presented to us as the best of all possible worlds, but whose dangers grow clearer and more urgent with each passing day.

The first practical measure that should be taken is to legalize competition. Restore to Americans their right to use precious metals as a medium of exchange—a simple and reasonable initial step if we believe in freedom. It is essential that Americans be given the chance to escape from this system and protect themselves from possible financial ruin, by being able to use gold and silver if they so desire. If anyone would rather continue to transact in the depreciating dollar, he would be free to do so. But anyone who prefers a currency that holds its value and won't become worthless before his eyes just because his government ran the printing press one too many times would have real options.

Right now, various disabilities make it difficult for gold to be used in market transactions. Sales and capital gains taxes on precious metals should be promptly repealed, and the enforceability of gold clauses in private contracts definitively reaffirmed.

What other policy for sheltering Americans from the collapse of the dollar is being advanced? Is there any, apart from comforting delusions that the Federal Reserve, which is itself responsible for our financial mess, can be trusted to put everything right? For one thing, how can we be expected to place so much trust in a Federal Reserve System we're not even allowed to audit? And even if the Fed chairman really possessed the singular genius our media and politicians regularly ascribe to him (no matter who he is), what if things have reached a point at which the Fed simply cannot stop the collapse? What if economic law, which the Fed can no more defy than it can repeal the law of gravity, is about to hit the Fed and the American people like a tidal wave, before which little rate cuts here and there are like the tiny umbrella Wile E. Coyote puts over his head to protect himself from falling boulders?

In other words, what if I and other sound-money advocates are right?

If we're wrong, then all we've done is eliminate some taxes on gold and silver. No harm done. But if we're right, we've given the American people a crucial safety net against financial collapse.

Tinkering here and there is not the solution, but as I've said, it is the only proposal Americans are permitted to hear. It is long past time that we begin asking fundamental questions rather than trivial ones, that we educate the people rather than distract or confuse them. Simply trying to patch up monetary problems after they've occurred, whether it is the NASDAQ bubble or the housing bubble, neglects to treat the root of the problem and must therefore fail. We cannot solve the problems of inflation with more inflation. We need to ask: *How did we get here?* What causes these bubbles? Financial bubbles simply happen, the political establishment tells us; these bubbles are an unfortunate but inevitable side effect of a market economy. That is nonsense. But it is convenient nonsense for some people, and that's why it gets repeated so often. It gives the perpetrators of the financial debacle that now confronts us a chance to get off the hook. We shouldn't let them.

CHAPTER 7

The Chickens Come Home to Roost

Just a few short months after the hardcover edition of this book appeared, the wheels started coming off the American economy. During the presidential primary season, people on the business networks often couldn't understand why I was sounding the alarm—wasn't everything booming? Yet we now find ourselves in what is shaping up to be one of the most severe economic downturns since the Great Depression.

That is, it *could* be one of the most severe if government chooses to make it so. When government stepped aside in the deep downturn of 1920 and allowed the market to correct all the malinvestments that had distorted the economy at that time, recovery was in full swing by the following year. On the other hand, when after the stock market crash of 1929 government imposed destructive price and wage rigidities on an economy that needed flexibility in order to make the necessary adjustments from malinvestment to healthy resource allocation, the result was a Great Depression that went on for years and years.

Unfortunately, the government's preferred solution to the

crisis today involves the very things that got us into this mess in the first place. We are in this crisis because of an excess of artificially created credit at the hands of the Federal Reserve System. The solution being proposed? More artificial credit by the Federal Reserve. No liquidation of bad debt and malinvestment is to be allowed. By doing more of the same, we will only continue to intensify the distortions in our economy—all the capital misallocation that occurred during the boom—and prevent the market's attempt to reestablish rational pricing of houses and other assets.

Ever since the 1930s, the federal government has involved itself deeply in housing policy and developed numerous programs to encourage homebuilding and homeownership. Government-sponsored enterprises Fannie Mae and Freddie Mac were able to obtain a monopoly position in the mortgage market, especially the mortgage-backed securities market, because of the advantages bestowed upon them by the federal government. Fannie originated as a government agency in 1938, and Freddie was established in 1970. They were later "privatized," but as usual, the partial privatization that actually took place was so perverse as to give privatization itself a bad name. The two mortgage giants had a special line of credit with the treasury, got special tax and regulatory advantages, and operated under the presumption (an accurate one, as events later proved) that the public would bail them out should they ever get into financial trouble. Some free market!

Add to this mix the Community Reinvestment Act, which, in the name of nondiscrimination, required banks to reduce their lending standards in order to extend more loans to members of demographic groups said to have been underserved by banks in the past. Cheap credit and loosened lending standards also encouraged people to buy houses on a speculative basis, confident that prices would continue to rise. They took out adjustable-rate or interest-only mortgages, with no money down. When things turned sour, they defaulted.

These governmental measures, combined with the Federal Reserve's loose monetary policy, led to an unsustainable housing boom. Eventually, economic reality finally set in: More houses had been built than could be sold at the ever-higher prices builders and sellers expected, and more and larger homes had been sold than people had the resources to pay for. The boom had not been built on a sound foundation of savings. It had been built on the sand of artificial credit creation. Imagine that: Wealth can't be created out of thin air by a central bank. It comes only from work, saving, and sacrifice.

Chapter 6 explains the Austrian theory of the business cycle. As we saw there, when interest rates are artificially lowered, borrowing money becomes much cheaper, and therefore longer-term and more capital-intensive projects, which would be unprofitable at a higher interest rate, suddenly seem profitable. A boom ensues. But this boom is artificial. It is based only on an increase in the supply of money, not real consumer demand. The result is malinvestment, a misallocation of resources into sectors in which insufficient demand exists. In recent years, this phenomenon manifested itself in overbuilding in real estate.

The bust in the housing market devastated the reckless Fannie and Freddie. In early September 2008 it was announced that Fannie and Freddie would be put into "conservatorship," a nice word for nationalization, which means the American people will pick up the tab for their bad loans. As everyone had expected, in the last resort the public was indeed on the hook for these institutions' foolish decisions after all. Practically the entire mortgage market was placed into government hands, and just about all we heard from politicians and the media was how "sadly necessary" it all was.

Oh, and here's a big surprise, courtesy of the *New York Times*, September 6, 2008: "Both presidential nominees expressed support for the government's plans to take over the companies."

The companies should have been put into receivership and their assets liquidated. Recklessness and mismanagement on such a scale would have been swiftly punished in the free market, which is why so many in the upper echelons of our economy, in their heart of hearts, are opponents of the free market.

Later in September we got the notorious bailout package, which sought to give the treasury secretary a $700 billion line of credit to buy up bad assets from failing financial institutions. (As I write this, the strategy in practice has been somewhat different, with the secretary instead buying stakes in banks themselves.) Virtually all of respectable opinion, in the media, among intellectuals, and within both major political parties, urged us that we had no choice but to pass it. It would save our economy.

Now whenever a Great Bipartisan Consensus is announced, and a compliant media assures everyone that the wondrous actions of our wise leaders are being taken for our own good, you can know with absolute certainty that disaster is about to strike.

The bailout package was not just economically foolish. It was downright sinister. It made a mockery of our Constitution, which our leaders should never again bother pretending is still in effect. It promised the American people a never-ending nightmare of ever-greater debt liabilities they would have to shoulder.

Two weeks earlier, financial analyst Jim Rogers said the bailout of Fannie Mae and Freddie Mac had already made America more communist than China! "This is welfare for the rich," he said. "This is socialism for the rich. It's bailing out the financiers, the banks, the Wall Streeters." This package only amplified Rogers's point.

On September 24 President George W. Bush addressed the nation about the financial crisis, five days before the House voted to reject the proposed bailout. (About two weeks later he spoke to us again, in a five-minute address. The Dow dropped 200 points during that five minutes—just a coincidence, I'm sure.) He assured us that his administration was "working with Congress to address the root cause behind much of the instability in our markets." Care to take a guess whether the Federal Reserve and its money creation spree were even mentioned?

We were told that "low interest rates" had led to excessive borrowing, but we were not told the truth about how these low interest rates had come about. They were a deliberate policy of the Federal Reserve. As always, artificially low interest rates distort the market. Entrepreneurs engage in malinvestments—investments that do not make sense in light of current resource availability, that occur in more temporally remote stages of the capital structure than the pattern of consumer demand can support, and that would not have been made at all if the interest rate had been permitted to tell the truth instead of being toyed with by the Fed.

Not a word about any of that, of course, because Americans might then discover the role of the great wise men in Washington in this great debacle. Better to keep scapegoating the mortgage industry or "wildcat capitalism" (as if we actually had a pure free market).

Speaking about Fannie Mae and Freddie Mac, the president said: "Because these companies were chartered by Congress, many believed they were guaranteed by the federal government. This allowed them to borrow enormous sums of money, fuel the market for questionable investments, and put our financial system at risk." Doesn't that prove the foolishness of chartering Fannie and Freddie in the first place? Doesn't that suggest government just might have contributed to this mess after all? And of course, by bailing out Fannie and Freddie, hasn't the federal government shown that the "many" who "believed they were guaranteed by the federal government" were in fact correct?

Then came the scare tactics. If we don't give dictatorial powers to the treasury secretary "the stock market would drop even more, which would reduce the value of your retirement account. The value of your home could plummet." Left unsaid, naturally, is that with the bailout and all the money and credit that must be produced out of thin air to fund it, the value of your retirement account will drop anyway, because the dollar will decline in value so much that it will barely buy you anything. As for home prices, they are obviously much too high, and supply and demand cannot reach equilibrium if government insists on propping them up. Houses are durable consumption goods, not investments or get-rich-quick schemes. Treating them that way, with the help of artificially cheap credit, made their prices skyrocket, putting them out of reach for a vast percentage of Americans.

If the president's speech was intended to rally people to the bailout plan—now being described inoffensively as the "rescue plan," a term the compliant media promptly adopted—it failed. According to congressional staffs, calls were coming in one-thousand-to-one against. My own office didn't get quite so many calls, but that's probably because most people already knew there was no way I would ever vote for such a boondoggle. Miraculously, on September 29, the bill failed to pass the House.

Washington refused to take no for an answer. Our victory and their defeat could not be allowed to stand. The Senate promptly passed a revised version of the bill, which was then sent back to the House. The House now voted yes. There was a sense of dreary inevitability about it all.

What happened in between the two House votes was that people with money started making calls. To many congressmen, that's even more important than a one-thousand-to-one against call ratio from constituents. Lobbyists called. Banking presidents called. Threats and scare tactics were used. Favors were called in, in exchange for previous campaign contributions. The vote then went the way they wanted.

As I said on the House floor, only in Washington could a bill demonstrably worse than its predecessor be brought back for another vote and actually expect to gain votes. The Senate version marginally reduced the treasury secretary's discretion, but the major change was the additional pork: $150 billion in handouts was the price for winning over enough House members to the plan.

Thus was our one-party system complicit in yet another crime against the American people. The very people who, with somber faces, tell us of their deep concern for the spread of democracy around the world were the ones most insistent on forcing a bill through Congress that the American people overwhelmingly opposed. The two major party candidates for president both voted for the bailout—another example of the big choice we were supposedly presented with last November: yes or yes.

The bailout package was little more than a form of price control, an attempt to keep asset prices artificially elevated. The root of our recent economic boom, as in any other business cycle, was government intervention in the market under the guise of lowering the interest rate, which is itself a price. To put it gently, politicians do not seem to know too much about the role that prices play in the market in equalizing supply and demand, and the distortions that necessarily accompany all government attempts at price-fixing. In order for the economy to return to normal, the Federal Reserve must cease the creation of new credit, the prices of overvalued assets must be allowed to fall, and malinvested resources must be liquidated or reallocated.

The government doesn't like this, however, and it undertakes measures to keep prices artificially inflated. One of the primary causes of the length and severity of the Great Depression in the United States was the federal government's attempts to do just that. Fashionable opinion had cause and effect reversed: Falling prices were said to have caused the Depression, when in fact the falling prices were the result of the economic depression, and were a necessary feature of the economy's return to a healthy and sustainable condition. Few politicians were listening to the few economists who bothered to point that out. Predictably, then, the Fed tried everything to introduce more artificial credit into the economy. The federal government took extraordinary measures to prop up prices. And the Depression went on for years and years. On the other hand, as I noted earlier, when liquidation was allowed to proceed unhampered in the equally devastating downturn of 1920, the economy had recovered by the following year.

You will not be surprised to learn that policymakers today

die, the purchase of the insurance giant AIG, and the "rescue plan" all have one thing in common: They seek to prevent the liquidation of bad debt and worthless assets at market prices, and instead try to prop up those markets and keep those assets trading at prices far in excess of what any buyer would be willing to pay.

By the time of the bailout package, the Federal Reserve had already injected hundreds of billions of dollars into U.S. and world credit markets. The adjusted monetary base was up sharply, bank reserves exploded, and the national debt had gone up almost half a trillion dollars in the previous two weeks. (By October, the national debt had already gone up a full one trillion dollars for the year.) Yet we were told that after all this intervention, all this inflation, we still needed an additional $700 billion bailout, otherwise credit markets would seize and the economy would collapse. This is the same excuse that preceded previous bailouts, and undoubtedly we will hear it again in the future after this bailout fails.

Where will the money come from? As of this writing the figure being thrown around is $850 billion, but since government always and everywhere underestimates how much its programs will cost, we can expect the final price tag to be much higher. The bailout will balloon the national debt and increase the amount of money we pay—already in the hundreds of billions—merely to service the interest on it. The only possible outcomes are crushing tax burden or the destruction of the dollar, which will devastate practically everyone.

In the immediate term, more debt and inflation are the strategies most in favor in Washington, since no one wants to impose as additional $850 billion in new taxes. When we add together the cost of all these bailouts, and add in the cost of all the new lending facilities the Federal Reserve has initiated, we are well an additional $850 billion in new taxes. When we add together the cost of all these bailouts, and add in the cost of all the new lending facilities the Federal Reserve has initiated, we are well into the trillions of dollars. More borrowing alone cannot begin to cover the cost. The Fed will create the necessary money and credit out of thin air, and wreck the dollar.

Ludwig von Mises noted that government interventions always produce consequences at odds with their intended effect—for instance, price controls on milk, designed to make milk more accessible, reduce the quantity of milk supplied and thus wind up making milk *less* accessible. Thus government typically seeks additional intervention, in order to correct the perversities caused by earlier interventions. There is no logical stopping point to this process of ever-more regulation—that is, until the economy is completely depressed and exhausted.

That's where we're liable to be if government keeps trying to fix the situation. It will create a worse crisis in the process of trying to avoid the current one. Instead of the brief 1920 downturn, we'll have something closer to 1929, that persists year after year despite—or, more accurately, because of—feverish government efforts to end it.

Additionally, bailouts and government guarantees encourage moral hazard of the worst sort. Now that the precedent has been set, what is to prevent the same thing from happening again in the future? (No, more "regulation" of the already heavily regulated financial sector won't solve a thing—after all, the regulators told us the mortgage market was fine!) Future bailouts, too, will be foolishly blamed on the free market, even though the free market, unlike the government, bails out no one and guarantees no one's profits. Once again, the congressional solution exacerbates and encourages the very behavior that gave us the crisis in the first place. We have no right to be surprised at still more reckless lending and irresponsible behavior on the part of financial firms in the future.

Bankruptcies cause pain, but they are not the end of the world. Physical plant, equipment, and the labor force all remain. Good assets are transferred into more skilled hands, and bad assets are liquidated. The bankrupt firm, which had been acting contrary to consumer wishes for some time, is no longer a drain on the productive economy. Bankruptcies are not easy, but how could the correction of the Fed's orgy of money creation have a painless solution? Postponing the inevitable—now *that* would be painful, as history has shown.

The only viable solution is to keep the government from intervening any further. The government and its central bank have done plenty to us already. By the time of the "rescue plan," the Federal Reserve had already lent hundreds of billions of dollars through its numerous lending facilities, and the Congress had passed legislation authorizing further hundreds of billions of dollars to bail out Fannie and Freddie. Each successive crisis event is advertised as larger and more severe than the previous one. And these crises will get worse and worse until the market is finally left to purge itself of all the bad debt and misdirected resources, and free up capital for use by more sensible entrepreneurs.

Famed investor Jim Rogers, when asked on CNBC what two things he would do if appointed Fed chairman, replied that he would abolish the Federal Reserve and then resign. People will say Rogers's answer was flippant. But times like these call for a return to fundamentals. If the federal government's takeover of private companies and its multitrillion-dollar bailout of Wall Street are just fine, how can anyone say with a straight face that a discussion of our monetary system, and whether it should be less manipulable by government, is out of bounds? Previous busts in American history were consistently preceded by artificial bank credit expansion of one kind or another, whether or not a central bank existed at the time. It's about time we looked into why that should be.[1]

The claim that the market caused all this, a claim obviously advanced in order to justify another round of government growth, is so staggeringly foolish that only politicians and the media could pretend to believe it. Nothing I have described in this chapter has anything to do with the free market. What led us to this crisis was moral hazard encouraged by government, massive monetary expansion brought about by government, and mortgage regulations forced on the private sector by government. But the idea that freedom caused the crisis has become the conventional wisdom, with the desired result that those responsible for the credit bubble and its predictable consequences—predictable, that is, to those who understand sound, Austrian economics—are being let off the hook. The Federal Reserve System has actually positioned itself as the savior, rather than the culprit, in this mess! What we need is an end to all this destructive government meddling in the market.

---

[1] Fears that a gold standard will cause "deflation," and that we therefore need a money supply the government can manipulate at will, misunderstand both gold and deflation. For more on this subject, I refer readers to the educational resources at CampaignForLiberty.com.

The willful misunderstanding of the causes of the crisis that we hear in politics and the media will be used to justify vast new powers for the federal government. That's why education is so important at this critical moment. And the points we need to make are really not so difficult. Reckless spending; reckless borrowing; reckless money creation; a reckless, trillion-dollar foreign policy; reckless entitlement growth—all of this could not go on forever. Individuals and nations alike must live within their means. Old-fashioned common sense is reasserting itself before our very eyes.

Chapter 8

The Revolution

I have heard it said that mankind does not want freedom, that people are happy to be slaves as long as they are entertained and well fed. I have likewise heard it said that most Americans have bought into the version of events they are given in the mainstream media and are perfectly content to be told what to think—what is good, what is bad, who is politically acceptable, who is politically unacceptable.

I don't believe this for a second. For one thing, our own American Revolution would have been impossible if this mentality had prevailed. Contrary to what many Americans have been taught, a majority, not a minority, of the colonists supported the fight for liberty against Great Britain.*

---

*John Adams is often misquoted as saying that one third of Americans supported the revolution, one third opposed it, and one third were indifferent. Historians have repeated this incorrect quotation time and again. Adams was in fact speaking of American support for the French Revolution. Historian William F. Marina has shown convincingly that a majority of Americans supported the American Revolution.

The fact is, liberty is not given a fair chance in our society, neither in the media, nor in politics, nor (especially) in education. I have spoken to many young people during my career, some of whom had never heard my ideas before. But as soon as I explained the philosophy of liberty and told them a little American history in light of that philosophy, their eyes lit up. Here was something they'd never heard before, but something that was compelling and moving, and which appealed to their sense of idealism. Liberty had simply never been presented to them as a choice.

We are engaged in a great battle of ideas, and the choices before us could not be clearer. I urge those who agree with this important message to educate themselves in the scholarship of liberty. Read some of the books I recommend in my reading list. Learn from the Mises Institute and Mises.org, the most heavily trafficked economics Web site in the world. Visit LewRockwell.com, an outstanding and crucially important Web site I visit every day.

I have devoted this book to ideas that I consider important, if typically neglected, if our country is to restore its former self. How much of my program could be accomplished in a presidential term, or in a decade or two, I do not know. But a bare minimum of what the successor to George W. Bush should seek to achieve? I suggest the following.

First, we need to rethink what the role of government ought to be, and fast. If we continue to think of our government as the policeman of the world and as the Great Provider from cradle to grave, our problems will grow worse and worse and our downward economic spiral, the first signs of which we are now witnessing, will only accelerate. The role of world policeman has made our country poorer and less safe. The welfare state likewise threatens our financial solvency and has caused the once-robust institutions of civil society—which are no longer needed when government performs all functions—to atrophy.

Right now our government is borrowing $2.2 billion every day, mainly from China and Japan, to pay for our overseas empire. As our dollar continues to decline, thanks to Federal Reserve inflation, the American debt instruments that these countries are holding lose their value. We cannot expect these and other countries to hold on to them forever. And when they decide that they no longer wish to, our fantasy world comes crashing down on us. No more empire, no more pledging ever more trillions in new entitlements. Reality will set in, and it will be severe.

Our present course, in short, is not sustainable. Recall the statistics: in order to meet our long-term entitlement obligations we would need double-digit growth rates for 75 consecutive years. When was the last time we had double-digit growth for even one year? Our spendthrift ways are going to come to an end one way or another. Politicians won't even mention the issue, much less face up to it, since the collapse is likely to occur sometime beyond their typical two-to-four-year time horizon. They hope and believe that the American people are too foolish, uninformed, and short-sighted to be concerned, and that they can be soothed with pleasant slogans and empty promises of more and more loot.

To the contrary, more and more intelligent Americans are waking up to the reality of our situation every day. Now we can face the problem like adults and transition our way out of a financially impossible situation gradually and with foresight, with due care for those who have been taught to rely on government assistance. In the short run, this approach would continue the major federal programs on which Americans have been taught to be dependent, but in accordance with our Constitution it would eventually leave states, localities, and extended families to devise workable solutions for themselves. Or we can wait for the inevitable collapse and try to sort things out in the midst of unprecedented economic chaos. I know which option I prefer.

No one who has learned to be dependent on these programs needs to be thrown into the street. But in the long run these programs are insolvent. If we do not begin a transition process funded by savings from our bloated overseas presence, everyone will be out in the street because the programs will simply collapse.

Americans were given an implied contract when they began paying into Social Security, so we should not want to strip away from them the resources they understandably anticipated receiving upon retirement. Contrary to popular belief, right now money for Social Security recipients comes not from some "trust fund" into which people have paid over the course of their working lives. If congressmen had voted the way I consistently have—I have never voted to spend a single penny out of Social Security—then we would not face nearly so serious a problem. The fact is, there is no money in any trust fund. The government spent it on other things. The money that retirees receive comes directly from current workers. Current workers are not building up a Social Security nest egg for themselves; they are giving their money to current recipients and hoping there will be enough workers to support *them* when *they* reach retirement age. But no part of the system involves paying money to the government and receiving that money with interest after a certain age. The government feeds into that illusion, but it is an illusion all the same.

I have long favored giving young people the right to opt out of Social Security, since such an option follows naturally from my belief in individual liberty. But since current Social Security recipients are being supported by tax receipts from current workers, how would those people be cared for if young people began opting out? The transition period should be funded by curtailing our overseas expenditures, which are not only out of control but have also compromised our real security interests by spreading our forces so thin. If we really oppose Big Government, we cannot make an artificial exception for bloated military bureaucracies, which traditional budget-minded conservatives never hesitated to look at seriously as a source of potential savings. As many empires throughout history have learned too late, more is not always better. In this way we can phase in the ideas of responsibility and self-reliance, commonsense ideas to which young people respond very favorably when I mention them.

In addition, the budgets of every federal cabinet department should at the very least be immediately frozen, a policy that all responsible people can surely embrace. Everyone should be forced to live within his or her means—all the more so when we are speaking of federal agencies for which the Constitution makes no provision. Most departments, with the exception of State, Defense, and Justice, deal with matters that our Constitution properly leaves to the states or to the people, and the people should no longer be exploited to support them. For too long, swarms of Washington bureaucrats have grown fat with wealth and power—all in the name of the "common good," they assure us—at the expense of the beleaguered American people. That must come to an end.

Forget all the protests we'll hear about how indispensable these departments are—departments Americans got by very well without for more than 80 percent of our history, I might add. We do not have the resources for them. That is the point. And more forced labor to fund them is neither morally acceptable nor economically wise.

It is only our intellectual inertia and lack of imagination that make us think these departments necessary in the first place. A federal Department of Education, for example, is an insult to the American people, who are more than capable of running their own schools without being looted to support a national education bureaucracy. We would get by just fine without it, as indeed Americans did for most of the twentieth century, a period when—by just a coincidence?—the population was far better educated than it is now. In fact, given the Department of Education's sorry record, if I truly opposed learning and knowledge I would propose tripling its budget.

If we adopted a sensible policy like this, the very announcement would restore strength to the dollar. And the more we lived within our means, the less inflation we would have and the less the poor and middle class would suffer, since there would be less pressure on the Fed to monetize debt.

We also need to begin to restore monetary freedom, which means that Americans should be free, if they wish, to engage in transactions and contracts denominated in gold and silver. It is essential that Americans be able to protect themselves in this way against any coming monetary disaster that would leave them holding valueless dollar bills. No one in politics or the media even talks about the issue, so you know it must be important.

There is much that the president cannot do on his own and that requires the approval of Congress. He may earnestly recommend certain courses of action, and try to rally the public behind them, but the initiative rests with Congress. Everything we have described in this chapter thus far falls into this category. At the same time, in areas critical to the health of our republic the president holds tremendous power for good in his own hands.

For one thing, every president sets priorities in the enforcement of laws and how he directs the attorney general. Just because the federal government has been given a power does not mean it must be exercised. The president could simply declare that the executive branch will direct no resources to the prosecution of medical marijuana patients. He could refuse to violate habeas corpus. He could refuse to detain people forever without legal counsel and without even knowing the charges against them. He can take these and other sensible measures even if Congress should refuse to curtail runaway executive authority, since the president is nowhere obligated to exercise such authority. And he can not only refuse to issue any more unconstitutional executive orders, but he can even issue an executive order repealing those that previous presidents have issued.

In foreign policy, the president as commander in chief can order the troops brought home from Iraq in a matter of months, not years, a policy no top Democratic candidate in 2008 consistently committed to. (Again, so much for the opposition party.) We are told by the war propagandists that such a withdrawal will lead to chaos, as if chaos did not exist there already, but these are the same people who also assured us that the war would be a breeze and that the whole thing would be paid for out of oil revenues. Why should we take their predictions seriously ever again? In the case of Vietnam, which is now a trading partner and has a functioning stock market, we have accomplished much more in peace than we ever did in an enormously costly war.

Particularly in light of the National Intelligence Estimate that was released in December 2007, the president should order the navy to back off the shores of Iran, and make clear that we have no intention of attacking that country. The president should likewise declare that the United States is abandoning its isolationist posture of refusing major diplomatic contact with Iran and that he is willing to talk with Iranian leaders, just as American presidents talked to Soviet and Chinese leaders throughout the Cold War. The sanctions against Iran should also be removed, as a further indication of our country's shift away from isolationism.

The price of oil would shoot downward and the dollar would move upward on the basis of these announcements. The United States would suddenly become diplomatically credible once again for the first time in years. The isolationism that our leaders have imposed on us would now be reversed, as our government once again observes basic norms of conduct to which all countries are expected to conform. No longer would the White House—which is now viewed throughout the world the way the free world once viewed *Pravda*, the old communist newspaper—bombard the international community with a ceaseless barrage of war-justifying propaganda that no one anywhere, apart from the gullible (and often complicit) American media, actually believes. And no longer would the patriotic sentiments of decent Americans be exploited on behalf of wars that have more to do with imperial ambition than with American security.

In other words, we need to keep our wits about us, and replace our bull-in-a-china-shop foreign policy with a statesmanlike approach that is appropriate to the real needs of American security. We also need to stand firmly against moral relativism, recalling that actions do not become moral just because our government performs them.

And if we really oppose isolationism, as all our politicians assure us they do, then sanctions against Cuba should be lifted as well. Sanctions hurt the target population but rarely do serious harm to the targeted regime. How well have our sanctions succeeded in getting rid of Fidel Castro, who has happily exploited the sanctions in order to posture as an anti-American martyr oppressed by Yankee wickedness? There is no reason that Americans should not be free to travel and trade with Cuba. When I said so in a Miami Republican debate, the response was not unexpected. Afterward, though, I spoke to a huge rally—with Cuban-Americans making up 70 percent of those in attendance—where everyone cheered the message of freedom. It seems to be a generational issue: younger people, not emotionally or politically attached to our failed policy, know the Cuban regime's days are numbered no matter what, and that freedom, as usual, is the most morally attractive position for America to take starting right now.

It is also time to begin bringing American troops home from around the world—an absolute necessity if the budget is ever to be brought under control. We're going broke and we still have 75,000 troops in Germany? Talk about being frozen in the past. The president should notify our allies of the policy, which no one ever told Americans was to be in effect indefinitely, and then begin a withdrawal. We have not had a foreign policy that is proper to a republic for many, many years, and it is long past time that we reestablished one. If we did, Americans would be safer, our military would be more efficient and effective, and we would make an excellent start toward restoring our international competitiveness—other countries, after all, are not burdened with the same self-imposed overseas expenditures with which the federal government has weighed down the American economy for so many years.

What I am describing is the only realistic option Americans have. (That is, it *would* be their most realistic option if anyone in our government would actually offer it to them.) The alternative consists of an ever-growing financial burden, more police state measures, and an endless string of wars, pitched to Americans on the basis of now-familiar propaganda and financed by more borrowing, higher taxes, and more money printed out of thin air. The collapse of the dollar will not be far behind.

The empire game our government has been playing is coming to an end one way or another. This is the fate of all empires: they overextend themselves and then suffer a financial catastrophe, typically involving the destruction of the currency. We are already seeing the pattern emerging in our own case. We can either withdraw gracefully, as I propose, or we can stay in our fantasy world and wait until bankruptcy forces us to scale back our foreign commitments. Again, I know which option I prefer.

Will it be difficult? Perhaps, though not nearly as much as some people think. We would finally begin to pull ourselves out from the crushing burden of debt and unfunded obligations that have hung over our economy for far too long. Our country would enjoy far more robust economic performance than we have seen in many decades. Rich and poor alike could once again look to the future with confidence, instead of a sense of foreboding.

Doing nothing would be far more difficult. In my travels around the country I have discovered that young people are waking up to reality faster than anyone else, since they realize that the cosmetic changes our political class is calling for will do nothing to prevent the financial catastrophe they now fear they will inherit. What decent parents would want to do such a thing to their children?

Ours is not a fated existence, for nowhere is our destiny etched in stone. In the final analysis, the last line of defense in support of freedom and the Constitution consists of the people themselves. If the people want to be free, if they want to lift themselves out from underneath a state apparatus that threatens their liberties, squanders their resources on needless wars, destroys the value of their dollar, and spews forth endless propaganda about how indispensable it is and how lost we would all be without it, there is no force that can stop them.

If freedom is what we want, it is ours for the taking.

Let the revolution begin.

Appendix

Ron Paul in the House Financial Services Committee, September 10, 2003.

Mr. Chairman, thank you for holding this hearing on the Treasury Department's views regarding government sponsored enterprises (GSEs). I would also like to thank Secretaries [John] Snow and [Mel] Martinez for taking time out of their busy schedules to appear before the committee.

I hope this committee spends some time examining the special privileges provided to GSEs by the federal government. According to the Congressional Budget Office, the housing-related GSEs received $13.6 billion worth of indirect federal subsidies in fiscal year 2000 alone. Today, I will introduce the Free Housing Market Enhancement Act, which removes government subsidies from the Federal National Mortgage Association (Fannie Mae), the Federal Home Loan Mortgage Corporation (Freddie Mac), and the National Home Loan Bank Board.

One of the major government privileges granted to GSEs is a line of credit with the United States Treasury. According to some estimates, the line of credit may be worth over $2 billion. This explicit promise by the Treasury to bail out GSEs in times of economic difficulty helps the GSEs attract investors who are willing to settle for lower yields than they would demand in the absence of the subsidy. Thus, the line of credit distorts the allocation of capital. More importantly, the line of credit is a promise on behalf of the government to engage in a huge unconstitutional and immoral income transfer from working Americans to holders of GSE debt.

The Free Housing Market Enhancement Act also repeals the explicit grant of legal authority given to the Federal Reserve to purchase GSE debt. GSEs are the only institutions besides the United States Treasury granted explicit statutory authority to monetize their debt through the Federal Reserve. This provision gives the GSEs a source of liquidity unavailable to their competitors.

The connection between the GSEs and the government helps isolate the GSE management from market discipline. This isolation from market discipline is the root cause of the recent reports of mismanagement occurring at Fannie and Freddie. After all, if Fannie and Freddie were not underwritten by the federal government, investors would demand Fannie and Freddie provide assurance that they follow accepted management and accounting practices.

Ironically, by transferring the risk of a widespread mortgage default, the government increases the likelihood of a painful crash in the housing market. This is because the special privileges granted to Fannie and Freddie have distorted the housing market by allowing them to attract capital they could not attract under pure market conditions. As a result, capital is diverted from its most productive use into housing. This reduces the efficacy of the entire market and thus reduces the standard of living of all Americans.

Despite the long-term damage to the economy inflicted by the government's interference in the housing market, the government's policy of diverting capital to other uses creates a short-term boom in housing. Like all artificially created bubbles, the boom in housing prices cannot last forever. When housing prices fall, homeowners will experience difficulty as their equity is wiped out. Furthermore, the holders of the mortgage debt will also have a loss. These losses will be greater than they would otherwise have been had government policy not actively encouraged overinvestment in housing.

Perhaps the Federal Reserve can stave off the day of reckoning by purchasing GSE debt and pumping liquidity into the housing market, but this cannot hold off the inevitable drop in the housing market forever. In fact, postponing the necessary but painful market corrections will only deepen the inevitable fall. The more people invested in the market, the greater the effects across the economy when the bubble bursts. No less an authority than Federal Reserve Chairman Alan Greenspan has expressed concern that government subsidies provided to GSEs make investors underestimate the risk of investing in Fannie Mae and Freddie Mac.

Mr. Chairman, I would like once again to thank the Financial Services Committee for holding this hearing. I would also like to thank Secretaries Snow and Martinez for their presence here today. I hope today's hearing sheds light on how special privileges granted to GSEs distort the housing market and endanger American taxpayers. Congress should act to remove taxpayer support from the housing GSEs before the bubble bursts and taxpayers are once again forced to bail out investors who were misled by foolish government interference in the market. I therefore hope this committee will soon stand up for American taxpayers and investors by acting on my Free Housing Market Enhancement Act.

A Reading List for a Free and Prosperous America

These are some of the books that have influenced me over the years. Naturally, some are more suited to the beginner than others. Some of the monetary texts, for instance, are for the advanced student, so I recommend beginning a study of monetary economics with Murray Rothbard's short book *What Has Government Done to Our Money?* (listed below), a classic that has been translated into countless languages.

ARMENTANO, DOMINICK. *Antitrust and Monopoly: Anatomy of a Policy Failure*, 2nd ed. Oakland, Calif.: Independent Institute, 1990.

BACEVICH, ANDREW J. *The New American Militarism: How Americans Are Seduced by War*. New York: Oxford University Press, 2006.

BAMFORD, JAMES. *A Pretext for War: 9/11, Iraq, and the Abuse of America's Intelligence Agencies*. New York: Anchor, 2005.

BOVARD, JAMES. *Terrorism and Tyranny: Trampling Freedom, Justice, and Peace to Rid the World of Evil.* New York: Palgrave Macmillan, 2004.

DiLORENZO, THOMAS J. *The Real Lincoln.* New York: Three Rivers Press, 2003.

ENGDAHL, F. WILLIAM. *A Century of War: Anglo-American Oil Politics and the New World Order.* London: Pluto Press, 2004.

FLEMING, THOMAS. *The Illusion of Victory: America in World War I.* New York: Basic Books, 2004.

————. *The New Dealers' War: FDR and the War Within World War II.* New York: Basic Books, 2002.

FLYNN, JOHN T. *As We Go Marching.* Garden City, N.Y.: Doubleday, 1944. Flynn, an accomplished journalist, analyzes fascism in Italy and Germany and concludes by considering the state of America in his day.

FOLSOM, BURTON W., JR. *The Myth of the Robber Barons: A New Look at the Rise of Big Business in America.* Herndon, Va.: Young America's Foundation, 1993.

GARRETT, GARET. *The People's Pottage.* Caldwell, Id.: Caxton, 1953. This is a persuasively argued and compellingly written early critique of the New Deal policies of the 1930s.

GIBBON, EDWARD. *The History of the Decline and Fall of the Roman Empire.* New York: Modern Library, 2003 [1776–88].

GRIFFIN, G. EDWARD. *The Creature from Jekyll Island: A Second Look at the Federal Reserve,* 4th ed. Westlake Village, Calif.: American Media, 2002.

HAYEK, FRIEDRICH A. *The Road to Serfdom.* Chicago: University of Chicago Press, 1944.

HAZLITT, HENRY. *Economics in One Lesson.* New York: Three Rivers Press, 1988 [1946]. This classic text has helped millions of Americans understand basic economics and the free market in just a few hours. (An indication of how the world has changed: Hazlitt once wrote editorials for the *New York Times*.)

HOFFER, ERIC. *The True Believer: Thoughts on the Nature of Mass Movements*. New York: Harper & Row, 1951.

HOLZER, HENRY MARK, ed. *The Gold Clause: What It Is and How to Use It Profitably*. iUniverse, 2000.

JASTRAM, ROY WILLIAM. *The Golden Constant: The English and American Experience, 1560–1976*. New York: John Wiley & Sons, 1978.

JOHNSON, CHALMERS. *Blowback: The Costs and Consequences of American Empire*, 2nd ed. New York: Henry Holt, 2004.

KWITNY, JONATHAN. *Endless Enemies: America's Worldwide War Against Its Own Best Interests*. New York: Congdon & Weed, 1984.

LANE, ROSE WILDER. *The Discovery of Freedom*. New York: John Day, 1943.

MACKAY, CHARLES. *Memoirs of Extraordinary Popular Delusions and the Madness of Crowds*. London: George Routledge & Sons, 1869 [1841].

MISES, LUDWIG VON. *Human Action: A Treatise on Economics*. New Haven: Yale University Press, 1949.

MUELLER, JOHN. *Overblown: How Politicians and the Terrorism Industry Inflate National Security Threats, and Why We Believe Them*. New York: Free Press, 2006.

NAPOLITANO, ANDREW P. *Constitutional Chaos: What Happens When the Government Breaks Its Own Laws*. Nashville: Thomas Nelson, 2006.

———. *A Nation of Sheep*. Nashville: Thomas Nelson, 2007.

PALYI, MELCHIOR. *The Twilight of Gold, 1914–1936: Myths and Realities*. Chicago: Henry Regnery, 1972.

PAPE, ROBERT. *Dying to Win: The Strategic Logic of Suicide Terrorism*. New York: Random House, 2006.

PASTERNAK, BORIS. *Doctor Zhivago*. New York: Pantheon, 1997 [1958].

PATERSON, ISABEL. *The God of the Machine*. New York: Putnam, 1943. A classic work of libertarian political theory.

POWELL, JIM. *Wilson's War*. New York: Crown Forum, 2005.

RAND, AYN. *Atlas Shrugged*. New York: Random House, 1957. I consider all of Rand's novels worth reading, in spite of my strong disagreements with her on important matters.

READ, LEONARD E. *The Love of Liberty*. Irvington-on-Hudson, N.Y: Foundation for Economic Education, 1975.

REES-MOOG, WILLIAM. *The Reigning Error: The Crisis of World Inflation*. London: Hamish Hamilton, 1974.

ROBERTS, PAUL CRAIG, and LAWRENCE M. STRATTON. *The Tyranny of Good Intentions: How Prosecutors and Bureaucrats Are Trampling the Constitution in the Name of Justice*. Roseville, Calif.: Prima, 2000.

ROCKWELL, LLEWELLYN H., JR. *Speaking of Liberty*. Auburn, Ala.: Ludwig von Mises Institute, 2005.

ROTHBARD, MURRAY N. *America's Great Depression*, 5th ed. Auburn, Ala.: Ludwig von Mises Institute, 2000.

———. *What Has Government Done to Our Money?* Auburn, Ala.: Ludwig von Mises Institute, 1990. The entire text is available for free at http://www.mises.org/money.asp.

RUEFF, JACQUES. *The Monetary Sin of the West*. New York: Macmillan, 1972.

SCHEUER, MICHAEL. *Imperial Hubris: Why the West Is Losing the War on Terror*. Washington, D.C.: Potomac Books, 2004.

———. *Through Our Enemies' Eyes: Osama bin Laden, Radical Islam, and the Future of America*, rev. ed. Washington, D.C.: Potomac Books, 2004.

SENNHOLZ, HANS F. *Age of Inflation*. Belmont, Mass.: Western Islands, 1979.

SOLOMON, NORMAN. *War Made Easy: How Presidents and Pundits Keep Spinning Us to Death*. New York: Wiley, 2006.

STERN, JESSICA. *Terror in the Name of God: Why Religious Militants Kill*. New York: HarperPerennial, 2004.

TANSILL, CHARLES CALLAN. *Back Door to War: The Roosevelt Foreign Policy, 1933–1941*. Chicago: Henry Regnery, 1952.

TOCQUEVILLE, ALEXIS DE. *Democracy in America*. Chicago: University of Chicago Press, 2002 [1835, 1840].

TUCHMAN, BARBARA J. *The March of Folly: From Troy to Vietnam*. New York: Ballantine, 1985.

WEAVER, HENRY GRADY. *The Mainspring of Human Progress*. Irvington-on-Hudson, N.Y.: Foundation for Economic Education, 1953.